CHASING SHADOWS
Memoirs of a Sixties Survivor

by
Fred A. Wilcox

THE PERMANENT PRESS
SAG HARBOR, NEW YORK

Copyright © 1996 by Fred Wilcox

Library of Congress Cataloging-in-Publication Data

Wilcox, Fred.
   Chasing shadows / by Fred Wilcox.
      p.   cm.
   ISBN 1-877946-75-3
   1. Wilcox, Fred.   2. Beat generation—Biography.   3. Authors,
American—20th century—Biography.   4. New York (N.Y.)—Social
life
and customs.   I. Title.
   CT275.W55824A3   1996
   974.7′104′092—dc20
   [B]   95-279
                                                                              CIP

First edition October, 1996: 1,500 copies

Manufactured in the United States of America

THE PERMANENT PRESS
Noyac Road
Sag Harbor, NY 11963

I dedicate this book to:
Ken, Jack, Wendy, Sarah, Adrienne, Tommy, Tinker, and
Kathy.

I would also like to thank Jenny Stein and Jimmy Laveck
for their kind assistance and support

"Men are so necessarily mad that not to be mad would amount to another form of madness."

—Pascal

"This is the night, what it does to you. I had nothing to offer anybody except my own confusion."

—Jack Kerouac

Sanity Hearing, December '61

In a windowless room, six very somber people are sitting around a square table, each with a legal pad, three ballpoint pens, and a cup of coffee. A very red-faced man stands at the head of the table, nose streaked with purple veins, tadpole eyes darting about in large dark sockets. No one speaks, and I can hear dust particles floating through the air. Sweat beading down my sides and my heart pumping furiously, wobbling, stopping altogether. A miracle. I can see, hear, and feel, but my heart is no longer beating.

Tadpole removes his glasses, twirling them round and round, then dropping them on the table. He clears his throat, squints at me, flops into his chair and jots a few cryptic notes on his pad.

"Today's date?"

Can't be an IQ test. Tell him.

"The time?"

Glance at my watch, give him correct time.

"A.M. or P.M.?"

Now he has me. Never can remember the difference.

"The place?"

This is really getting monotonous.

An immensely serious-looking woman is examining my ears. She flutters her right hand, and I bend toward her, thinking it might feel rather nice to have her stroke my ears. Tadpole is scribbling in his notebook, knitting his brow in tight, angry folds. His jaw twitches as he writes. My feet itch, and I feel rather sleepy.

"Just let me ask you this," says a young intern with a large hair-sprouting mole on one cheek. A tortured pause. Well, spit it out man. What are you waiting for?

"Are you . . ." he trembles."Would you call yourself . . . I mean, is it true that you told Dr. Kinkno that you are a beat . . . a beat . . . nik?"

Smile, say nothing, determined to make him suffer.

"A . . ." he stammers again, the blasphemy burning his tongue, "AAAAA. . . . BBBBB. . . . Be. Bet . . . At . . . NI . . . KKKKKK?"

The writing ceases. Miss Ear Fetish winces, obviously fighting off a desperate urge to fondle one of my lobes.

"Oh, yes," to myself. "I'll confess. Jack Kerouac is my closest friend. We've criss-crossed the country together on freight trains, chewed peyote in the Mohave, chased Nirvana through the Himalayas. Ginsberg? Known the man since we were kids. Smoked hash with him in Algiers, rode angels through Mexico City together, helped him write Howl. Diana DiPrimas is my lover. Gregory Corso, Lawrence Ferlinghetti, Kenneth Patchen, William Burroughs, Kenneth Rethrox, are all my pals. Dig Miles Davis, love Charlie Mingus, been grooving on Lead Belly, Howling Wolf, Lighting Hopkins, Bo Diddly, since I was five years old, man."

"Am I a BBBBB. . . . . Eattttt. . . . . nKKKKKK?" I tease. "Yes, doctor, I'm afraid I am."

The intern stares at me for a long moment, then bends into his pad, writing with such fury that the hairs on his facial mole begin to dance. A bone-starved RN nods toward the heavens, folding her hands over her hollow chest and bowing her head with studied melodrama. Tadpole leaps to his feet, his long nose quivering like a divining rod and his glasses slipping to the floor..

"Goddamn it," he sputters, kicking his glasses across the room. "You are a little wiseass, aren't you? Ever since you came to Fairlawns you've been causing trouble, trying to tell people how to run this hospital. Well, you're no doctor and you never will be. Oh, you're smart all right. Too damned smart for your own good. Your mother was right to keep you in here. You'll never go back to school. Never hold a job. And you're gonna spend the rest of your life in custodial care. Because in my opinion you're NINETY FIVE PERCENT SICK. NINETY-FIVE PERCENT."

I am beginning to worry about his heart, and wishing it might give out.

"Excuse me, Tadpole," I reply, softly, not raising my voice, "but if I were ninety-five percent sick we wouldn't be having this conversation. I know where I am, who I am, and why I'm here. I'm here, quite simply, because I've already been here. Simple. Once you've been in, you sneeze at the dinner table and presto, back you go. I'm here, doctor, because there's no such thing as a 'former mental patient.' And I know the difference between a trial and an Inquisition . . ."

But Tadpole has stormed from the room, smacking his pad on the table and knocking the door closed. Out of all the doctors and nurses I've encountered these past two years he is definitely the most dangerous. At Fairlawns his word is absolute. With one flourish of his pen he can send you back to the streets or, handcuffed and tossed into the back seat of a sherrif's car, ship you on down to the snakepit. At Fairlawns, Tadpole is judge and jury, his sentences final. To argue or complain is futile. It is all quite legal, all done in the name of the people, on behalf of the state, to assure good order. There is no appeal, except perhaps to God, who doesn't intervene in these matters. I glance at my watch. The entire episode took less than five minutes.

CHAPTER 1

Going into Exile

"Who? Who is it I'm talking to? Who's there?"

"Flemington, is that you? Can you open the door. I'm wet. Really soaked."

"Who?"

"Don't you remember? From the university. I tried to call you. Couldn't find a phone that worked. Just walked down from the bus station. I wrote . . ."

The speaker goes dead. Old newspapers cling to the doorway. Candy wrappers, napkins, and cigarette butts litter the floor. On the landing, behind the smoky glass panel of the second door, someone is screaming:

"Well, he's not one of my 'boys', that's for sure. He must be one of yours, Flem . . . ing . . . ton."

"Oh really? One of mine? Just what does that mean? What might you be insinuating? What slander this time?"

"You know, Miss Fleming."

"I don't know, Miss Rock-riquez."

"Oh, you don't?"

"Listen, bitch . . ."

"I'll call the cops, Flemington. You know I will."

"Call them. They'll come and take you away to Bellevue where you belong."

"I really wouldn't be so sure, you little swish."

"Size queen."

"That's it, Flemington. That's . . . it . . . I'm calling the police . . . the landlord . . . You're out . . . it's back to Bellevue, or Forty-Second street for you, baby . . ."

Laughter. Slamming doors. Silence. The smell of stale garbage, marijuana, rancid beer.

"Flem, are you there?"

I push through the door, climbing the narrow stairs, feeling my way along a dark landing, past two or three doorways and into a tiny, poorly lighted room cluttered with boxes, piles of paper, books, and clothes. A path leads from the doorway to a foldout bed on which Flemington perches, eating something out of a paper container. I stand just inside the doorway, waiting to be invited to sit down. Flemington glances at me once or twice and continues eating.

He would march into our domitory's dining room, wearing a black cape and tapping his umbrella as he passed tables crowded with hungry students. "God," he would cry, "how can they expect us to dine with crocodiles? So ill-mannered. So," shuddering, "savage." After dinner we would gather in his room to drink Dubbonet and gin, and to listen to him recite passages from *Breakfast at Tiffany's*, "one of the most brilliant works of the twentieth century." Between recitations, he sucked on a long silver cigarette holder, regaling his audience with tales of mint juleps and ménage à trois, incest and eccentricity, madness and murder in his native, Faulknerian Mississippi.

I had written to Flemington, telling him I planned to escape from Clarion and would soon be coming to New York. "My door is always open," he replied. "Please know you will be most welcome here."

"Flemington? Is that you?"

"Of course, who did you think it would be, Captain Hook?"

"Well, I just arrived a couple of hours ago. Tried to call you. Bus took twenty-four hours. How are you?"

His eyes are sunk deep within their sockets, heavy-lidded, flat.

"They've turned off the electricity, so don't expect me to cook. What's so funny? I forgot to pay the bill, that's all."

"Nothing, Flem. I just thought . . . well, I guess I didn't expect . . ."

"Who really gives a damn what you expected. The thing is, I really can't ask you to stay here for more than a day or two. You see," waving his chopsticks about the cluttered room, "I'm terribly busy. And . . . oh God, why? Why must I explain everything to you? There now, set your valise right over there. Yes, that will be *your* own little corner. You can make," smiling and conducting with his chopsticks, "a nest over there. Nothing permanent, mind you. Everyone in New York wants to live . . . somewhere . . . Many, it now appears, right here . . . But I do not allow permanent nests in my home. Don't you see," bending forward in his chair and whispering into his cupped right hand, "people do come and go. Appear and disappear, always clamoring for a nest. But they shan't have mine. I've incurred some debts, and acquired a few enemies . . . but . . . this little nest, squalid as it may appear to YOU . . . is . . . MINE. Besides, I don't want the police here, do you understand? My nerves just aren't up to it."

We sit in silence, Flemington cocking his head from side to side, as though trying to listen to his visitor's thoughts. Sirens. Glass smashing in the airshaft. The humming of a space heater. Flemington, eyes still closed, struggling from his chair, threading his way through piles of rubbish, dialing and whispering into the phone's receiver.

The bathroom is tiny, but warm and safe. I wash my face, brush my teeth, the mirror steaming over. Mother was in bed with a migraine headache when I left. Tiny wands of light threading through the blinds, probing her mouse-colored hair, tapping her miniature nose. A vaporizer spitting out medicinal clouds. A clock ticking heavily. The furnace rattling. Doors slamming downstairs. The wands of light lacked magic; she didn't turn into a princess. "Mother," I whispered, standing away from the bed. "I'm going now. I have to catch a bus." Her eyelids were damp and veiny, and her eyes sea blue. No, that's hackneyed. Irish? When Irish eyes are smiling.

When I was a little boy I picked huge bouquets of daffodils from a neighbor's yard and gave them to her. "*M is for the million things she gave me. O means only that she's growing old. T is for the times she tried to . . . T is for the times she tried to tell . . . Put them all together they spell MOTHER, a word that means the world to me."* Eyes blue as . . . crocodiles . . . blue as . . . horsewhips . . . blue as . . . Mary Magdalene . . . blue as . . . Christ's wounds . . . blue, surely, as a mother's suffering.

"I can't see you, come closer." The hand rising, fluttering, falling. "You're really going?"

"Yes, mother, I"m going."

"And you have everything?"

"Yes, everything."

"Clean underwear, socks, your toothbrush?"

The wands were fading. She adjusted the covers, sighed heavily, examined the back of her right hand for a moment.

"You're sure?"

"Yes."

"Will you be coming back?"

"Of course."

"When?"

"I don't know . . ."

"Will you find a job . . . ?"

"Sure."

"But, where will you live? What if something happens. What if you get hurt or you're sick. We won't even know where . . . or how to help . . . if you're killed . . ."

"I'm not going to get hurt, and if I get killed, well, I won't be very concerned about calling you then, will I?"

She sobbed once, twice, opening her eyes and quickly closing them again. I bent down and kissed her on the forehead. "Dad is waiting in the car. Goodbye," I said. "I've got to go now." She did not reply.

The bus was idling, its windows opaque with grit. I bought a one-way ticket to New York City and stood waiting beside my father. We had fought with words and with our fists. He had called me sick, and I called him stupid. He mocked my desire to write poetry, and I laughed and told him he was illiterate. He said I wasn't a man. I replied that he was a lousy father. He told me to pray, I reminded him that God was dead, the universe empty, his faith a form of superstition.

I wanted to be back frying catfish with my dad on a sandbar in the Des Moines river, great flashes of heat lightning, a scimitar moon, our campfire glowing on the slow-moving black water, and waking before dawn to the aroma of bacon and eggs on winter mornings, our guns cleaned and oiled and inserted, with great care, into their cases. For two years I carried an unloaded .410 shotgun through ditches and fields and woods, my dad watching every motion, pointing out mistakes, praising the right movements, training me in the proper use of a deadly weapon.

We moved through tangles of frozen cornstocks, guns held in the crook of our arms, threading our way into ditches filled with glass-hard weeds and THUMPSWOOSH, a pheasant squawking wings pounding, my dad pumping his .20 gauge, the bird spinning wide-eyed with surprise to the ground. My father sliced open the quarry's stomach, shook its steaming guts onto the snow, and stuffed the bird into his field jacket. We crunched on, into the arctic wind, over barbed wire fences that sang like coyotes, passing mysterious hieroglyphics in the snow, studying tracks that stopped midstep, as though mouse or rabbit had learned to fly. My warrior hero leading the way, teaching me the things that his father and his father before him had taught boys who wanted to become men.

And then one morning in a windswept cornfield, cradling my shoutgun under my arm, a headless rabbit bleeding in the snow at my feet, I knew that I didn't want that anymore. Like my belief in God, the excitement of the hunt faded, inexplicably, away.

"Dad," I said.

"Yes?"

I wanted to say that deep down under layers of anger and hurt and self-pity were memories of trolling for pike on a Canadian lake, nights drinking good Canadian beer, telling stories by the fire, just the two of us in a small wooden cabin listening to the rain on the tin roof and the flames dying in the cast-iron stove, curling into our sleeping bags, the wind gently slapping at the windows, great fish leaping toward the stars, we could hear them.

"Well, so long dad."

"Goodbye, son."

We shook hands and I boarded the bus. I had lied to my mother and father, telling them that I was simply going on another adventure, that after chasing a few more shadows I would return to school, finish my degree, get a job and settle down. I did not tell them that the Greyhound was an immigrant ship, setting sail for the new world, taking me into exile. Not for a week or a month or even a few years, but for the rest of my life. The bus choked once or twice and began to move. I waved; my father wasn't there.

Flemington is sitting on the couch, apparently asleep. The buzzer rings, and he leaps to his feet, yanking off the chain lock and throwing open the door. A man in a black trench coat waddles into the apartment, blinking and twisting his head about like a bewildered groundhog.

"Oh, I see," he groans, waving one chubby hand toward me.

"No you don't, Paul," Flemington shouts. "No . . . you . . . don't . . ."

"A guest?"

"No one," Flemington replies, "no one I really know anyway."

"I see," the man sighs. "I do see, Flemington."

Flemington drapes his cape over his shoulders, kicks a path through piles of books and papers and laundry, stops:

"Don't make any long-distance calls," he warns. "And under no circumstances should you answer questions from my creditors. If anyone comes to the door, tell them I'm recently deceased, and you're the new tenant."

I stay in Flemington's nest, sleeping until late afternoon, then scribbling in my diary or composing poems until it is too dark to write . . . High on Ritalin and beer, I travel the city, absorbing its sounds, adopting its inflections and rhythms. Buildings tower over me, subways roar beneath my feet. Behind a million curtains, families are sitting down to dinner, schoolchildren are doing their homework, men and women are complaining about their jobs, couples are making love.

Just weeks ago, I stood by the barred windows of Clarion State Hospital, my heart pumping rage instead of blood to my brain, planning my escape, plotting my getaway not just from the snakepit but from my family, my friends, my home-town, home state, everyone and everything I had ever known. Sooner or later I would walk out of there, either on their terms, or mine, it made no difference. Hatred would be my friend, my confidant, my source of inspiration. Anger would fuel my dreams, feed my hunger, fill up my lonliness, instruct my vision, inspire my poetry.

I ride the subway for hours, getting off at random stops and wandering past vacant lots crammed with battered, burned-out cars, past buildings that lean out over the side-walk, as though trying to shake the people inside out into the street, past children playing hopscotch and stickball and people sitting on stoops, drinking wine and smoking reefer, staring with bitter indifference at this poor dumb white boy looking for drugs or sex or God-knows-what-action, but this is Harlem, motherfucker, not Nebraska, this is the Bronx, not Iowa, you stupid whitebread faggot. So drunk one night that I wet my pants following three pimps toward their prom-ise of "free hot pussy" into a dank little cave where they punch and kick me, ripping my clothes open with their switch blades while the bartender watches t.v. and I stumble into the street, calling to a mounted cop that I've been robbed, I've been rolled, I've been beaten, and the cop bends far over the grand neck of his very grand horse. "Are you the guy from Ohio that's been causing all the trouble around here lately?" he shouts. "Take a hike, o.k., before I take you in."

I fill out an application at the New York State employment agency, hesitating when I reach the last two lines:

Have you ever been in a psychiatric facility or mental hospital? If so, please explain.

"Something you don't understand?" the interviewer asks.

"Oh, no, just a mote in my eye."

The interviewer is a middle-aged woman, black horn-rim glasses hovering on the hump of her large nose, pink fin-gernails, rhinestone fish hanging from her ears. She says "youse" and "da" a lot, and she is very kind.

"Do you have an address?"

"Sort of."

15

"A phone?"

"Not really. I mean, Flemington doesn't like . . . well, no."

"Can you type?"

"Yes, very well."

"Why don't you go back to college? I see you've finished three semesters?"

"Well, my mother got sick, and my father passed away, and my sister is an alcoholic, and I just couldn't afford . . ."

"Couldn't you borrow?"

"No."

"No one in your family would help?"

"No one in my family has any money."

"I see, but you dropped out of college more than a year and a half ago. Whaddya been doin' all dis time? I mean, if we send you to an employer, they're gonna want to know dat. It's really not good to have these big gaps in your work history, ya know? Particularly if youse can't explain what ya been doin'."

"I've been working," I lie.

"Why don't youse fill in that part?"

"They were just temporary jobs. Youse know," I say, starting to imitate her accent. "Diggin' ditches. Washin' dishes. Spent a little time as an orderly in a psychiatric hospital, ya know?"

"Oh," she says, her hand brailing across my application. "Must a been rather tryin' work."

"Yeah, very tough."

"I had an aunt who was sick once."

"Sick?"

"Yeah. Thought she was Emily Dickinson."

"The hermit of Amherst?"

"Wrote some big paper on Miss Dickinson, studied everything dere was ta know about her life, ya know, and couldn't draw the line between herself and . . ."

"Did she write poetry?"

"Yeah, but it was bad. Sounded terrible."

"How did you know that?"

"It was just silly, that's all."

"Because she was crazy?"

"No."

16

"All poets are crazy, aren't they?"

"Well, my aunt really believed . . ."

"What did you do with her?"

"We had to, well she couldn't, I mean we weren't able . . ."

"You locked her up?"

"Sort of."

"Put her in the nuthouse?"

"A facility."

"Right, a facility."

"That's what we called it."

"Why didn't you just call her Emily?"

"Emily?"

"Did she ever write anything like this?"

> *Because I could not stop for Death,*
> *He kindly stopped for me;*
> *The carriage held but just ourselves*
> *And immortality.*

"Yeah, sad things like that, always about death and things."

"Maybe she really was Emily Dickinson."

"What?"

"Nothin'."

The interviewer shuffles through a stack of cards and, removing one, smiles.

"I've got it. You're from Idaho. You must know a lot about trees, am I right?"

"Iowa."

"Whatever, but trees, right?"

"Yes, I know a lot about trees."

"Youse go up to the Parks Department. They're lookin' for supervisors, someone who knows all about trees, to help spruce up the city for the World's Fair."

The job turns out to be little more than standing on street corners, or sitting in bars, watching Italian laborers smash holes into sidewalks, dig down a few feet, and toss in a London Plain tree. I'm supposed to make sure that the holes are at least two feet deep, that the trees have a three-inch circumference, and that the crews don't chop through any gas or water mains. We plant trees across 125th Street, up and down Lenox Avenue, back over into Spanish Harlem. The workers ignore me, pretending not to understand English when I wrap my little tape measure around a tree and, finding that it's too thin, demand they send it back to the nursery in New Jersey. The foreman buys me breakfast and lunch every day, hoping to distract me from doing my job.

"After all," he says, "no tourists in their right fucking mind are gonna visit this neighborhood. Why should they? What's to see here, anyway? Trees look nice now, but the dogs are gonna piss on 'em, people'll smash into them with their cars, the junkies will dig them up and try to sell 'em, or chew off their bark hopin' to get high. Why bother? These people don't appreciate nothin'. Don't work for a livin', and don't give a shit about their own neighborhood, so why should we? Hey, live and let live, that's my motto. No sweat off my balls as long as I get paid. Fuck 'em if they can't take a joke, right?"

I walk through Harlem, a briefcase stuffed with blueprints under my arm, trying to look important. When I stand on the sidewalk watching the workers dig, people stop to stare, to chat, or to curse me. "Mother Sands" waves her hankey over each new hole, chanting and singing—she sounds a lot like Billie Holliday—for the "soul of these little baby trees." I give her fifty cents for each blessing and she says a little prayer for my soul too. A gang strolls by, dressed in identical coats, stopping, staring at me, then at the workers in the hole, back to me. "What the fuck, man," their leader demands. "I mean, you're white, that why you're not down there diggin' in them holes? Why you plantin' trees around here anyway? How come trees, man? I don't see no fuckin' swimmin' pool, do you? Kids swim in trees? We eat trees? Pay the motherfuckin' rent with trees? Fuck your trees, man. I say FUCK your trees, you dig?"

I tell them that I'm just working for the city of New York, and they shrug, spit, stare hatred into my bones. I tell them that I'm just tryin' to earn some money, that I don't own the goddamn trees, or the sidewalks, or the city. "Fuck you," I say with my own eyes, staring back at them until their leader steps forward, nose inches from mine, eyes burning. I watch his hands, waiting for the move and suddenly he is laughing.

"Forget this shit, man," he says. "Leave the cracker alone. He cool, man. He be real cool."

After work I stop into Stanley's, a Lower East Side bar I stumbled into during one of my late-night rambles through Manhattan. A cluster of old beats sit by the window, stroking their ancient mustaches and beards, waiting for Godot or Kerouac or some voyeuristic kid from uptown who's dying to screw poets who refuse to remove their shades, even while they're balling chicks. The old beats arrived in Stanley's shortly before the birth of Jesus, and now they sit by their window, sipping Pernod and watching the parade of aspiring bohemians parade along Avenue B. Late afternoon and the fledglings pour in, shoving out the Polish drunks who snore, heads on their arms, at the bar. Stanley's wife, a swollen goose egg perched on the edge of her stool, swills down oceans of vodka. She yawns, derisively, at the screwballs who love her bar. Exiles, fugitives, and chasers of shadows squeeze into Stanely's. The old Mandarins sit by their window, regal, distant, and almost always drifting out the door and away down Avenue B with some precious young thing in black tights, a brand new beret, handmade leather sandals, the real McCoy shades, and a blond mane that falls to the tip of her horsey swinging Long Island hips.

The bartender flirts with me, buys me drinks, and introduces me to other patrons. His name is Alfie and during his break he takes me upstairs to his pad, shrugging and laughing and offering me a joint when I say no to his advances. "Oh hell, honey, it was worth a try, wasn't it? I figured you weren't gay, but you are cute, that's for sure. No offense. Let's be friends. I just can't help it. I get so horny around this time of month, you know, right before my period."

Alfie's roommate and "sort of" lover is an expressionistic painter who works exclusively with dark colors, creating portraits of gang members and street boys on huge, eight-by-ten canvases. He turns his models into fierce creatures with giant gargoyle heads and claw-like hands and feet. "Oh, yes," Alfie giggles. "Miss Morgan does have quite an imagination, doesn't she? Reminds you of the painter Munch, don't you think so? He has this rather morbid thing about gang members. You know, anyone who looks and acts really really bad.

Of course, his true motive is that he wants to *do* them, or have them *do* him, but meanwhile he paints them . . . with their clothes on . . . Poor little Morgan. So mixed up. He had a mad love affair with his own sister all through high school. Their parents would go out to dinner and Morgan and sis just raced into the bedroom, ripped off all their clothes, and had sex for hours. My goodness, and now he likes tough little boys. Has a rather one-track mind, though I would say he has some real talent, don't you think?"

We return to the bar, and Alfie introduces me to a man who claims to be a warlock and wants to know, leaning into my ear, if I have five thousand dollars to invest in "acid." "Never heard of it?" he laughs, draining the drink I've just bought him. "It's LSD. And I tell you, it casts a strange spell. A lot more fun than alcohol. Everyone down in D.C. is doing it. Jackie and her friends are wild about it. Even JFK. So if you can get five thousand dollars we'll buy a few thousand tabs, truck on down to Washington, come back with a load of cash." I tell the warlock that I don't have five thousand cents and he giggles, asks for another drink, and says he wants to sleep under my bed tonight. "Give you good vibes," he promises. But I don't have a bed, just a corner in Flemington's nest, and I'm about to lose that.

Flemington appears at odd hours, rushing in at 2:00 a.m., rummaging through papers, scribbling notes, counting out things, and stroking the walls as though searching for some hidden door. He appears startled to see me, and only mutters "Yes, to be sure," or "Indeed" when I attempt to talk to him. He paces about for hours, muttering, making phone calls, throwing himself in a dramatic heap on the bed and snoring for a while before slamming out the door. One morning Flemington returns in a jovial mood. "Here," he laughs, handing me a twenty-dollar bill. "You look positively famished. For God's sake go out and buy yourself something decent to eat."

When I return from breakfast, Flemington has already changed the locks on his door and I can hear him rummaging about inside his nest, singing an aria from one of his favorite operas, but he refuses to answer my knocking, and

I walk to the Lower East Side and sit in Tompkins Square Park, watching the pigeons and winos and junkies, steam rising from the styrofoam cup warming my hands. Count. Count: $6.94. Count again: $6.98. The city wakes, commences its daily roar. Pigeons peck, squirrels scramble, dogs romp, fledglings shuffle by, scratching their heads, rubbing their drug-swollen eyes. The tree planting job has ended, a park bench is my new home. The city wakes, and I move into its flow, carried along by the excitment of nine million people swimming together in this frenzied little bowl.

I will sleep on tenement roofs and park benches, in junkie crash pads and abandoned lofts. The police will smack the bottom of my feet with their nightsticks and when I awaken blinking and dazed they'll order me to get the fuck down the street. I will fear them more than the gangs, the muggers, the junkies, the angry spades, more than anyone on the city's mean streets.

I curl catlike and camouflaged into dark corners, one eye open, ready to spring knife-in-hand at mouse sounds, startled by the rustle of a rat's whiskers, shaken by a pigeon stirring in its sleep. Waking stiff-kneed and happy to be alive, a coyote gnawing through my guts, pulling them up and out through my esophagus and I can smell-taste the coyote's meal and kneeling beside him I stroke his carnivorous ears and whisper kind things while we breakfast, together, on my own, empty, insides.

Des Moines, 1961.

To my family, I am Gregor Samsa, the young civil servant in Franz Kafka's story who turns into a huge bug. An ordinary choir boy who kisses his parents a perfectly normal goodnight, only to appear as a strange and repulsive creature in the morning; a dutiful son who goes off to school with a Bible under his arm, only to return home shouting "God is dead, the universe is empty, and life is absurd, I believe in nothing."

The beatnik graduate assistants I bring home from college prop their unwashed, sandal-clad feet on the table, guzzle my father's beer and recite passages from Frederick Nietszche. They turn pencils into chopsticks, thrusting them into the Sunday pot roast, dribbling mashed potatoes down their bearded chins, belching loudly. Over dessert, my Kerouacian pals demand to know if my parents "really dig free sex," whether they might like to "stoke up on a little hashish," and if they've ever had "Reichian orgasms." Do they realize that if God is dead, anything is possible. If God is dead, man must be God. The graduate assistants laugh into the silence. I laugh too.

I am driven by an insatiable curiosity, a feeling that I must absorb all of the world's knowledge, must see, feel, and experience everything. I can't sleep, barely eat, ignore my studies, burn with some strange new energy. Walking through the streets at night I don't just observe a cricket, I become the cricket. Acorns speak to me, but I don't merely listen to them germinate. I enter the ground, take in water, absorb sunlight, feel my brittle shell expanding, my small green center reaching for the sun, breaking through the soil, emerging, growing year after year until my limbs are strong enough to hold treehouses and tire swings, and I scatter orange and yellow leaves in autumn and sing ribald operas when the wind blows, and . . .

Is it really madness to become a cricket or an oak tree? To feel the pain of animals smashed beside the road? The ones who administer the tests, prescribe the cures, and attach electric spurs to my head say it is manic to become a cricket, manic to talk of being an acorn, manic to argue with the moon, crazy to discuss philosophy with squirrels, sick to lie naked in the wet grass and not think or read or discuss but just BE ecstacy.

Manic, they insist, must be assuaged, ameliorated, relinquished, modified, transferred, sublimated, structured, made useful, reasonable, sensible, constructive, fashionable, normal. Parents must not allow their children to be manic. Teachers must report manic. The state must pass laws to regulate manic. New tests must be developed to detect manic at an earlier age. Operations for manic. Pills for manic. Laws against manic. Jail cells for manic. Hospitals for manic. STOMP OUT MANIC. Don't let your son or daughter become a cricket. Report signs of your wife or husband becoming an acorn. Arrest naked humans who talk to the stars. WAR ON MANIC. LAUNCH OPERATION MANIC. Weed them out, round them up, tie them down, lock them away, don't let them vote, keep them out of public places, deny them tenure, revoke their licenses, sterilize their offspring, strip their citizenship, send them to Siberia, DOWN oh ever so DOWN with manic.

CHAPTER 2

Mean Streets

In *winter, when they lay piled on the sidewalks, their turnip-colored ankles hugely swollen, blood frozen on their lips and inside their noses, infected scabs on their foreheads, it is difficult to tell if they're alive or dead. But in warm weather they rise up, slowly stretching their feeble arms and legs, yawning, scratching their sides. I like to sit with them, sharing rotgut and hardluck stories, waiting for the mission to open for lunch.*

"Have you ever had Syph-i-lis?"

"No."

"Louder please."

"NO."

"Have you ever had Tu-ber-cu-lo-sis?"

"No."

"Speak up."

"Hell NO!"

"Have you ever had He-pa-ti-tis?"

"NO NO NO."

"Have you ever had Jaun-dice?"

"NO."

The doctor has only two fingers, and three inch-long stubs on each hand. He wears blood-stained cheesecloth mittens over the stubs, speaks with a thick East European accent, and snaps us with a rubber band every time he asks a question. He snaps us on the chest, stomach, face. "Have you ever had . . . ?" Snap. And? Snap snap. Have you? Snap snap snap. He lifts our shirts, pokes one of his icepick fingers into our solar plexus, snap snap. He presses his stethoscope against our chest and listens to the soggy murmuring inside. Snap. Hepatic coughs. No, snap snap. Tubercular wheezing, NO NO NO NO, snap snap. Yellow blood-burst eyes, venereal incoherence, livers sauteed in wine, kidneys fried in gin, cerebellums parboiled in canned heat. NO NO NO, snap. The doctor snaps us with his rubber band, nodding in unison with our lies. In the doorway, two workers are giving the boot to a soot-covered skeleton. His forehead is caked with blood and his bare feet are rotting. He pleads and curses.

"You don't have to push me, goddamn youse."

"This is the third time you've been here in a week Benny. You tryin' to kill yourself or what, Benny?"

"I need money. I gotta eat like anybody else. I gotta find a place to sleep tonight. I need . . ."

"Benny, take a hike, Benny. We're takin' blood here, not poison Benny."

Benny hobbles across Second Avenue, calling curses down on the world. A man in a wrinkled blood-spattered smock sticks our index fingers with a needle, demands ID. We hand him wrinkled, expired driver's licenses, pawnshop receipts, a payroll stub plucked from the garbage, pilfered draft cards, wine-stained social security cards, patchwork welfare stubs, anything with someone's name and address on it.

"See that guy over there," says the man in the abbatoir smock as he pretends to write our pseudonyms in his logbook. "He's got a piece of paper bag with his name on it. That's all. Now, how am I supposed to know who he is? Comes in here twice a day, and twice a day we toss him out. Piece a bag. Guy could disappear, just blow away, nobody'd know. Nobody'd care. All right, you got A positive. Take a seat. Be patient. They'll call your number in a little while."

Rows of us now. Bruised, stinking, scabby, singing, cursing, praying, semi-conscious, unconscious, and with abrupt efficiency the men in white smocks jab needles into our forearms, thrust the needles into plastic tubes, connect the tubes to plastic bladders that squeak and wobble and splash and fill with blood. No hepatitis, no tuberculosis, no syphilis, no gonorrhea, bladders sloshing, the wino on the third table over passing out, and a man walking the rows, yanking needles, thrusting crisp five-dollar bills into shirt pockets or outstretched hands. Our blood will be sold to hospitals for fifty dollars a pint, transfused into the veins of grateful patients.

Lightheaded from selling blood twice in one week, I sit on the sidewalk, stretching my legs and pressing my back against the wall. Heat rises from Second Avenue, sucking air from my lungs. My head is wrapped in gauze and my shirt is Scotch-taped to my skin. Blood trickles from the tiny hole in my arm. Sweat stings my eyes. An old wino uncaps a bottle of Thunderbird, gulping twice and sighing with pleasure before offering it, without comment. I accept, without comment, tilting the bottle three times before returning it. Loud snapping in the blood bank, silent snapping in my empty stomach, the wine helping to anesthetize my hunger. Another swig and the old man drops the empty bottle on the sidewalk, wobbles off toward the Bowery.

When I threatened to kick in Flemington's door, he just laughed. "Go ahead, sweetpea," he called, "and you know where you'll be. Right back in the loonybin, if I need but remind you?" I had confided in Flemington, telling him that I was afraid my family would come to New York, that they would convince the police to pick me up, and that I would be shipped back to Clarion for the rest of my life. I told him that I had nightmares in which Dr. Hotchkins was lowering his electric spur to my head, grinning while my body flopped convulsively on the table.

Shortly before Flemington locked me out, a young beatnik took me to a loft where off-off-Broadway shows were performed. We scaled a brick wall, jimmied a window, and jumped inside. It was dark and warm and smelled like sawdust. We made love on a pile of costumes, and later Siobhan said the loft belonged to a woman who was touring southern France. "Her dad was a big time writer. He died two years ago, leaving her a trust fund, but she's cool. She won't mind if you crash here for a while."

Every night I scaled the wall (the door could not be opened from the inside without a key), hoping the police wouldn't arrest or shoot me. After washing up a bit in the bathroom sink, I piled civil war uniforms, tuxedos, and ballroom dresses into one corner, uncapped a quart of beer and settled into my soft little nest. The streetlights cast weird shadows on the walls, turning long racks of costumes into troupes of dancing ghosts and I would lay there, watching the performance, my eyes adjusting so that I could see very well in the dark. My ears became giant antennas, picking up every sound within and outside the loft, sorting out nuances, registering warnings.

I would lie awake for hours, feeling snug and secure. No one except the beat, who had disappeared shortly after we made love, knew where I was. No one. If the building burned the fire department would find an anonymous bundle in the ruins, one hand clutching an empty brown bottle. If someone crawled in through the window and slit my throat, no one would identify my body. I would lay there for weeks without a heartbeat, my eyes fixed on these spooky walls.

Yet I did not feel at all sad because the loft became my magic carpet, floating through a universe known only to me. I could travel to any galaxy I wished, and I could be a film star, a writer, a cowboy or war hero. I could wrap my imagination around hunger and loneliness and homelessness, turning a can of sardines into a gourmet dinner, making a few lines scribbled on a scrap of paper into a great book, transforming this cluttered loft into a castle. I could make love to beautiful women and win prestigious awards. I even returned to Clarion State Hospital, where, with just the touch of my hand, I snapped little Jimmy out of his evil spell, gave sight to the blind girl, brought a tiny old woman back to life. I could survive the night.

One morning I sensed some danger. It was July and I was sleeping naked in my loft oven, a hunting knife lying close to my side. I opened one eye just wide enough to make out a figure standing over me. The figure was holding something large and heavy, and before I could decide what it might be she threw a pot of cold water in my face. "What are you doing in my loft?" she shrieked. "Naked. Naked in my loft. What? How dare you? My costumes. Balling chicks on my costumes. Did you get any jissom on my costumes? Did you? You better not have. Goddamn you, sleeping on my costumes. Goddamn you." On and on, demanding that I get the blah blah out of her theatre, get the blah blah off her property before she called the blah blah and had my blah blah thrown in jail.

I tried to tell her that I was a poet, not a blah blah. That just like her own father had done, I was trying to put words to paper . . . A little down on my luck at the moment, but . . . This only made her scream louder, hurling the pot and an arm load of costumes at my head, rushing about the loft, muttering "goddamn" and blah blah a couple of thousand times before I could dress, dry my face on a satin evening gown, and flee.

I stash the five-dollar bill next to the hunting knife in my workboot. On the Bowery, men and women sprawl alone and in groups, reeking of cheap wine and sweat. Winos wait in line to sell their shoes and winter coats, even their trousers. The buyer leans against a light blue Cadillac, engine running, doors and trunk open, tossing shoes, pants, coats, hats, belts, socks, wallets, inside. A toothless woman pulls her dress over her head and waves it in front of the buyer, but he shakes his head, then turns his back on her. "What's the matter?" she taunts. "What's the matter? Last night you wanted me bad. What's the matter? I suck your little dicky doo you'll give me money, won't you shyster. Suck it yourself, shyster."

A wino strolls away in his underwear, grinning and clutching a dollar bill. The buyer pays 25 cents for a pair of pants, 75 cents for a decent pair of shoes, a dollar for a winter coat. They will take the money to the nearest wine store and sit on the curb, half naked but happily chugging paint-thinner wine, the coup de grace for some, the very last assault on their cirrhotic liver, hardened kidneys, ulceric duodena. In the morning a city truck will cart the dead away to paupers' fields on Welfare Island, placing them in wooden caskets, piling the caskets six high. There will be no markers. In a few years a bulldozer will scrape their bones into a pile to make room for others. Ashes to ashes, dust to dust. No trace. The phrase has a nice ring. "No trace, no trace" I sing, passing through Tompkins Square Park, down Avenue B, across 6th Street to a tenement between C and D.

Siobhan opens the door, barefoot, blinking out of sleep, and wearing a rumpled tee shirt from which her arms protrude like small, half-developed beans. Her apartment, two miniature rooms and a bath, is even more squalid than the crash pads where I often sleep, curled between two heroin addicts. It smells worse than the Bowery. Siobhan is a pack rat, a compulsive collector. In the middle of her living room floor is an old, ragged, mattress, a life raft in a sea of moldy magazines and newspapers, seashells, beads, bottles, bright colored pieces of glass, feathers, books, papers, balls of string, tin cans, pots of half eaten beans, crusts of green-coated bread, frying pans with the remains of last week's, or last month's dinner, bits of soap, records, dog bones, umbrellas, yarn, strips of ribbon, plates crusted with dried egg and tomato sauce. In the middle of all this sits a grizzly bear chewing on an old shoe. Siobhan calls him Puppy and refuses to walk him more than once a week. His huge demented eyes fix upon some dream forest when he squats in his favorite corner; his droppings litter the house.

Siobhan's father wanted to write the great American novel and, like many young writers, he expected instant fame and fortune, but instead the family's houseboat broke loose during a hurricane, Paddy's manuscript was lost, and his wife ran off with the family dentist. The poor man took to drink and let his children go hungry. His starving horses were put down by the SPCA. Siobhan threw a poker at him during a quarrel, then fled barefoot into the snow. Daddy had her committed to a state mental hospital, where she was givin forty insulin and fourteen electro-shock treatments.

In a small windowless office, Siobhan recounted her story to a welfare worker. She told the worker that she could never go home again, that she was living on the streets, and that she was hungry.

"Do you have an address?" asked the worker.

"No," said Siobhan.

"We'll need an address before we can help you."

"But I don't have any money."

"Yes, I know, but we need a mailing address."

"I've been in a mental hospital, and I can't work."

"I understand that, but were you declared psychotic?"

"I don't know."

"Can you substantiate that you can't work?"

"I can't, that's all. I don't have any place to live, or any clothes."

"Do you have a document showing you are mentally ill?"

"No."

"Any cash on hand?"

"Fifty cents."

"Will your father help you?"

"I told you, no."

"Do you use alcohol or drugs?"

"No."

"You're not a junkie?"

"No, I don't use drugs."

"No relatives or friends?"

"An older man uptown lets me sleep under his table."

"Well, the women's shelter is full right now. Can we call you?"

"I don't have a phone."

"A place to leave a message."

"I don't know."

"Good luck."

"Thank you."

When she isn't out looking for treasures, dressed in a Joan of Arc potato sack and even in winter without underwear or shoes, Siobhan burrows into her nest, reading Wilhelm Reich, Sigmund Freud, Otto Rank, Rollo May, and Eric Fromm. She keeps a diary on giant rolls of newsprint, scratching out several yards of microscopic notes each day and then cutting her work into pages which she stuffs into a pillowcase. Siobhan knows how to ride the subway without paying, where to score free clothes, and where to eat for free. She walks to the Fulton fish market, collects a bag full of fish heads and mixes them with vegetables to make chowders and stews. She climbs into supermarket dumpsters to gather half-rotten vegetables and fruits, cutting off the bad parts, using the good.

Sometimes we eat at the Catholic Worker, where we get heaps of good food and you don't have to sing or pray for your meals. We sit down with blood-caked winos, beatniks with huge goblin eyes, soot-crusted anarchists, delirious poets, starving painters. We stuff food into our mouths, chewing and gulping and loudly smacking our lips and then we sit outside on a park bench, holding our aching stomachs and chatting with the Bishop, a volunteer at the Worker who claims he's about to become the next Pope.

"Come on, Bishop, do you really think they're going to make you the next Pope?" Siobhan teases.

"Oh my yes," he replies. "I don't just think. I *know* they will. That's why I have to get my things in order. I'll be leaving here soon for the Vatican, very soon, for the ceremony in Rome."

I feel dizzy, the bad rush from cheap wine or bad pot, but at least the coyote isn't chewing on my insides. Siobhan's sack dress is stretched to upper-thigh and she is sitting with her legs wide, strumming an invisible guitar and singing, "I ain't sayin' you treated me unkind, you mighta done better but I don't mind, you're just kinda wastin' my precious time, don't think twice cause it's all right." On the way to the Worker, we passed a very thin, hump-shouldered young man with his arm around a strung-out hippie chick.

"Know who that is?" Siobhan asked.

"No," I replied.

"That's Bob Dylan. I caught his gig in the village the other night. I got in free. He's really great."

"What's he do?"

"He's a folksinger."

"I hate folk music," I said.

Siobhan's landlady collects the rent from her Puerto Rican tenants, going door-to-door when welfare checks arrive. The tenants aren't aware this is illegal, so they don't object when she cashes the checks on Avenue D, deducting deposits, fines, and fees, then returning a few dollars to each family. Her husband sits on the stoop, mumbling songs into a little black book. In the middle of January, when bitter winds slash off the Atlantic, he turns off the heat in Siobhan's building, sometimes for days, sometimes for an entire week. Even the rats in the hallway slow down, their greedy little eyes gone to marble, their legs paralyzed by the cold. Tap a garbage can and they topple off the sides. One day Siobhan and I are sitting in her kitchen. The oven is turned on full-blast and we are wearing our coats. Puppy is lying between our chairs, steam rising from his nose. Crystals of ice have formed on the bathroom window, and the sound of hollow coughing rises from the airshaft, echoes in the hallways, rattles through the walls. Just below Siobhan's window a man is screaming. I pry the window a few inches (it can't get much colder inside) and press my ear to the opening.

"Hey man, what does it say in that goddamn book about killing children? Does it say you have a right to murder babies? Does it? Does it tell you to freeze people to death, you fucking scumbag."

"This is my property," the landlord shouts. "Mine. You have no right to be here unless I say so. I . . . say so. You will be in jail for threatening me."

"Who's threatening you, motherfucker? Who said anything about a threat? I just asked you a question, that's all. So call the cops. I'll be in jail, and you'll be in hell." The man laughs, "Or wherever you're gonna go when YOU die, man."

"Why do you hate me?" the landlord cries.

"You're a piece of shit," the man replies, no longer shouting, his voice dangerously calm. "I don't know nothin' about hatin' you. I don't care nothin' about hate. I don't hate nobody. But a man comes in here and turns off the heat, and my children coughin' their guts out night and day. That's all. Seems like somebody tryin' to kill my kids, that's all I'm sayin'. That's it. Don't give me no hate shit, you fucking little weasel."

"Police," the landlord screams. "POlice."

"PO-LEEEECE," the man mimics. "Call him, motherfucker. Call the man. I'll tell him to arrest your ass for attempted murder."

When I return a week later the heat is still off, and the children are hacking even louder, dressed in coats, hats, and mittens, sitting in their kitchens by the oven. The hallway is strewn with garbage and smells like natural gas. Someone has urinated against the wall, and there are frozen puddles at the bottom of the stairs. Siobhan leaves her door unlocked, and Puppy greets me with a great wet kiss. She is in bed, covered with blankets and several coats she's collected on her walks. Cockroaches scurry across the floor, squishing under my boots. The walls and ceiling in Siobhan's bathroom are caving in and her bathtub is filled with a two-inch layer of plaster. She calls the city's hotline. "Someone will be right over," a man's voice promises. I call the hotline. "Sure, soon, real soon," says a soothing woman's voice. Live wires poke through the plaster, absorbing moisture, deadly to the touch. Siobhan thinks her landlord lives in Brooklyn, but she doesn't really know his name. No one ever shows up from the city to inspect Siobhan's bathroom. The rats grow fatter and more bold.

Late at night, drunk and with nowhere else to sleep, I pry open the battered door to Siobhan's building and stand in the hallway, listening to rats rattling in the garbage cans, the drip drip of water from the ceiling. I take my knife out of my boot and listen. There is no light in the hallway. The landlord refuses to repair the socket. Rattle. Drip. "O.K., motherfucker," I scream, waving the knife. "I'm coming in." I move cautiously down the hall, waiting to be attacked, but tonight there are no muggers, only the soft wispy rustle of rodent feet, a child's hollow coughing, a baby crying, a bottle smashing in the airshaft, and the steady gnawing of ten million cockroaches eating their way through the plasterboard walls, through copper, steel, and porcelain, through blood, brain, and marrow. Prehistoric, resilient, omnipotent, malevolent, invincible.

Summer arrives, and the slumlord's wife wears a low-cut cotton dress. She deducts the rent and fines from her tenants' checks, stuffing bills between her breasts. Without a word, a man yanks the dress over her elbows, spilling the landlady, and spreading the money into the street. The slumlord's wife crawls along the sidewalk, clutching at her torn dress, grabbing money and sobbing. "Animals," she hisses. "You are all animals. I hope you die, you goddamn ANIMALS." No one tries to take the money, and no one helps her pick it up.

Someone puts a nickel in the candy store's jukebox and the children commence to dance to the Temptations. Siobhan dances with Puppy. The landlord's wife crawls along the sidewalk, scooping up money. "Sugarpie baby, can't help myself, I love you and nobody else." Skinny kids, skunky winos, runny nose junkies, hungry dogs, mean-eyed cats, and even a few rats popping and tapping, grooving together in the street.

Siobhan and I lie naked on the life raft. She is reading passages from *Civilization and Its Discontents*. "Present-day civilization," she reads, "gives us plainly to understand that sexual relations are permitted only on the basis of a final" (I stroke her thighs) "indissoluble bond between a man and woman; that sexuality as a source of enjoyment for its own sake is unacceptable to it; and that . . . ." (lower myself between her legs) "its intention is to tolerate it only as the hitherto irreplaceable means of multiplying the human race." She continues reading. Puerto Rican boys are watching from the rooftop across the street. "Do it man," one of them shouts. "Get it on." They clap their hands and dance in a line, so close to the edge of the roof it feels like they are going to jump into bed with us.

The apartment bakes. Puppy licks my back. In the street below the children place a large rubber doll under newspapers, with just the head protruding, then they jump back to the sidewalk. The driver hits his breaks, skids, stops inches from the baby's forehead. When he sees the children laughing, and realizes they are booing him, he takes off. The children wait. A cab screeches around the corner from Avenue B, heading toward C. The cabdriver sees the baby in the street but doesn't slow down, hitting the head full speed, sending papers and baby's head flying toward the sidewalk. The children clap, shout, whistle their approval. They place the baby back in the street, booing when a car stops or moves slowly around the doll, cheering when a driver crushes their baby's head. Someone puts a nickel in the candy store's jukebox, punches the Supremes, and the children dance, waving their skinny arms, grinning, shaking their little asses. Siobhan and I slide across the mattress, keeping time to the music, to the children's laugher, to the cheers of the Puerto Rican kids on the roof. "I'm going to have a baby," she will say in January. "And you could be one of three fathers."

At night it is as hot, or even hotter, than midday. Manhattan is one giant steaming dumpling. Water gushes from hydrants, forming pools in the streets in which the children lie, poking their heads out like baby hippos. Cigarette butts and beer cans float on top of the pools. Police turn off the hydrants, people turn them right back on. Night is filled with explosions, sirens, singing, angry shouting, arguments. The city bakes. Without air conditioning—which no one in this neighborhood can afford—there is no relief, inside or out on the street. The city is on fire, sucking the oxygen out of the air, out of our lungs, and out of our brains. People walk the streets with heads lowered, desperate for relief, ready to gore anyone who gets in their way. The bodegas sell out of beer. No more ice. No one selling air. Tenants stick their heads out of windows, gasp like drowning fish, drag blankets and mattresses out onto the fire escapes, turn on feeble little fans that swirl the heat from one room to the next, fill bathtubs with water that quickly turns from tepid to warm. They climb to rooftops and tilt their heads skyward, as though trying to suck cool air out of the stars, spread out blankets and sheets, too miserable to worry about junkies or muggers.

Siobhan sleeps. I place my few belongings—a Gillette razor, pair of underwear, bar of soap, couple of books—into a paper bag. She'll understand, because she too disappears into the great asylum without a roof, chasing her own shadows up and down the island, returning to her nest with bags of treasures which she spreads across the floor, combing through and cooing over bits of junk, her precious pearls.

When I have money I bring Siobhan bags of groceries. When I don't, I steal from her to buy alcohol. Junkies squat on the sidewalks, slobbering, scratching, nodding. Siobhan invites them in and they sleep in her kitchen, in the bathtub under the falling ceiling, on the floor, their heads propped up with copies of *The Mass Psychology of Fascism,* and *The Complete Works of Sigmund Freud,* their faces half buried in garbage. They prowl through the apartment, stealing everything worth more than a dime. Siobhan throws them out, but they return, reppeling down the airshaft on ropes, scaling the sides of her building with their suction cup hands and feet, floating from rooftop to rooftop like flying squirrels.

They tie up their arms and shoot smack or speed into their veins, eyes rolling out of focus, heads bobbing, slipping into a deep slobber scratching nod. They pass out on the fire escape, vomit on the kitchen floor, and turn various shades of death, always riding the thin line between superhigh and overdose. We drag them into the bathroom, slapping them in the face, rubbing ice on their heads, screaming at them not to die. We lower comatose forms into the tub and turn on the shower, blasting cold water into the blue-cheese face of some nineteen-year-old kid from Minneapolis, and the deceased begins to moan, opens his eyes, blinks, smiles. Risen from the dead, the creature stands on wet wobbly legs, brushes back its hair, stretches its arms, coughs once or twice and asks:

"Anybody got a fix?"

One night Captain Garbage (he likes to get high on acid and stare into the bottom of a garbage can) is tying a piece of plastic tubing around his upper arm, a dim glimmer of expectation in his burned-out eyes. Puppy is watching the captain with rather bored approbation. Siobhan is asleep in the other room. Captain takes out his works—spoon, syringe, nickel bag of heroin. He melts the powder and fills the syringe.

"But what fun is it, Captain?" I ask. "All you people do is shoot up and pass out. Shoot up and sleep. You don't talk. You don't eat. You don't even fuck. You kill people to get that little bag of powder. And all it does is knock you out. How can you have fun if you're not even awake?"

"My friend," he sighs, finding a vein and driving the needle home, "I've been watchin' you, man. And I gotta tell you. I just gotta 'cause I'm your good friend, man. You're an alkie. A juicehead. Listen here, now. Someday that booze is gonna kill you, man. Someday drinkin's gonna do your sorry ass in."

I try to argue with him, but Captain's on his roll, his eyes glazed, head down between his knees and then, with the needle still dangling from his arm, scratching his fleas, he falls unconscious or dead to the floor.

I check his pulse, put a copy of *The Complete Works of Freud* under his head, snatch the five-dollar bill at his feet, and give Puppy a few loving pats.

"Dear Siobhan," I scribble on a piece of garbage bag. "You mighta done better but I don't mind. We never done too much talkin' anyway. Don't think twice cause it's all right. Love, Bobby D."

Observation & Evaluation, Des Moines, '60–'62.

At Wilberforce, a psychiatric hospital whose ivy-covered buildings, towering oak trees, and landscaped lawns give it the appearance of a small private college, the old men cry and wet their pants and the orderlies stuff rags into their mouths, tie their hands to the rungs of chairs, and slap their faces. One afternoon I refuse to sand boards or cut up women's panty hose, activities Wilberforce calls "occupational therapy". Instead, I visit a young psychiatric intern from Mexico who has soft-brown eyes and a lilting voice touched with sadness. Unlike other psychiatrists whom I've had the misfortune to meet, he is neither arrogant nor downright stupid. He doesn't want to know how many times a day I masturbate, and whether I want to have intercourse with my mother, kill my father, mate with or eat my siblings for breakfast. He doesn't try to force me to swallow experimental drugs, and he never threatens to send me back to the shock ward.

But even when I vow to tell the world about abuses at Wilberforce Sanitorium, Dr. Cordova refuses to investigate my charges. I am not allowed to use a phone, I do not have an attorney, any one to whom I might turn for help. I am, de facto, a mental patient. Habeas corpus does not apply to people in here. We cannot post bail. Can't cop a plea. Don't know when our sentences might be up, if ever.

"Would you like to see what goes on in cottage 6?"

"I cannot do that."

"Why?"

"I am only new here."

"So you're a prisoner too, just like the rest of us?"

"You are not a prisoner."

"Can I just walk out of here?"

"Well, I don't know that."

"Will you call the police?"

"Someone might."

"Why am I here?"

"Your mother wants you held for observation and evaluation."

"But I've been 'observed and evaluated' quite a few times already. Why don't you bring my mother in here? Why not 'observe and evaluate' her?"

Dr. Cordova shakes his head, laughing as though I've just told a very funny story. A pair of squirrels are playing hide and seek outside his window, chattering and flying from limb to limb. We smoke in silence.

"Do you think I'm crazy?"

"No."

"Do you think I have brain damage?"

"No."

"You know that my mother insists that I do."

"The tests show nothing like that."

"So I'm not crazy and I don't have brain damage. Then why don't you sign me out of here?"

"Because . . ."

"Because I've been locked up before . . ."

"Well, that is true."

"Do you know that the orderlies smoke marijuana, pop benzadrine, swill vodka, that they scream at us, threaten to beat us, and make us eat out of a wooden trough like pigs, sometimes with our bare hands?"

"No," says the Mexican intern.

"Are you aware that they torment the old men by refusing to allow them to go to the bathroom, and forcing food down their throats? Do you know this goes on here?"

He does not know.

"Do you think that being in Wilberforce will help anyone feel less depressed?"

He cannot say.

The squirrels stop playing and it begins to rain. Red and yellow leaves float to the ground. Thunder rattles the windows and light-

ning bounces across the sky. I stub out my cigarette. Dr. Cordova's children smile from inside gold frames. I smile at them. "Welcome to America, hombres."

"What?" Dr. Cordova asks.

"Nothing. Just a little joke between me and your children."

Dr. Cordova and I shake hands and I walk back through the rain to cottage 6 where the orderlies are preparing our dinner, slopping cans of kennelration onto metal plates. When we finish eating, they order us to line up for the evening search. Later, after we brush our teeth and put on our pajamas, I sleep with my head under the pillow, trying to drown out another night of drunken arguing and boisterous fucking in the kitchen of cottage number 6.

CHAPTER 3

Playing House

A tiny cafe in the south Village, checkered table-cloths, prints of
Venice and Florence on the walls, and I order chicken tetrazzini and
a glass of house burgundy, happy to be inside out of the rain, at a
table, eating, and the voice drones, "Yeah, so we took Anthony for a
ride. He was crying. We drove him out to Bayonne and blew his
face off. We stuffed a fish in his mouth."

Cursing in the corner of the cafe, men huddling around a radio,
the brims of their hats pulled down over their faces, fat tummies bent
into the table, chubby hands cupped to their ears. Their pounding
makes the silverware dance and the waitress places my salad down
the way one might lay a bouquet of flowers on a casket. "So we played
baseball with Niki's skull," the man continues. "So we took Sammy
for a ride and shot out his eyes. So we hammered Joey's kneecaps off
his legs." I finish my chicken tettrazini. "So I agreed to murder
Anthony Hands because Johnny Bones said that Frankie the actor
told him that two-fingered Paulie wanted Vito the shooter to stop
skimmin' off Tommy Two Guns' profits."

I drain my wine and pay the bill and the waitress smiles, and the
men in the corner pound on the table, and no one else comes in.

The sun is a gift, running its fingers through my hair,
massaging my scalp, caressing my face. Puppy curls beside
me on the park bench, muttering and whimpering in his

sleep. His fur glows honey brown and is warm to touch. I trace my hand along his back to the hole where the first slug entered, passing straight through and out the other side, the next shot lodging beneath his right eye, which is swollen closed and drains yellow mucus. When I press antibiotics into the bullet hole his good eye fills with tears and his head wags softly, a grieving Cyclops.

The babushkas squeeze onto benches, coats buttoned to the neck, bright colored scarfs wrapped around their heads, their feet laced into heavy black shoes. Tonight their husbands will take up accordions and commence to play as exiles crowd into the dance hall, swilling vodka, arguing, dancing, one old survivor drawing his bowstring across a fiddle, tentatively at first, then picking up the pace and the dancers will shuffle with a kind of determined, melancholy joy. And the next afternoon they will be back in the Vazac, eating raw fish sprinkled with paprika, pounding down shots, and falling asleep at the bar. Later, when the Wehrmächt blitzkriegs across the television screen in some World War II documentary, the exiles will slam their glasses on the counter, screaming and cursing and weeping until a commercial breaks into their rage.

Fat greasy pigeons stroll along the sidewalk, snatching up crumbs. A golden retriever with a red bandana tied around its neck romps into the birds, and the babushkas stare at the dog's owner, a tall bone-thin boy wearing a tattered cape. His eyes sag prematurely old in a badly pockmarked face, his bare feet are coated with dirt and running sores, and a small python curls over his neck. He steps up to the babushkas, grins, shuffles, sings, "How many dawns must a man travel down," strumming an invisible guitar, "before they will call me a dog." Bowing to the old Polish women, he lights up a joint.

"Yo," he says, spotting Puppy. "What's happening, man?"

"Nothing Zarro, we're just sunbathing," I say.

"Yeah man, that's cool. I mean, a dog sunbathing. Wow. Heard about his gettin' shot. Not cool man. Not cool at all."

"He's gonna live."

"Yeah. He's a badass dog for sure. But say man, you been up to Harlem lately? You scored? I could use some smack but the cops stopped me last night over on C and I'm standin' there holdin' my arms out and they're checking for tracks but ain't findin' none and I'm laughing so this cop says 'Hey, motherfucker, somethin' funny?' And I couldn't stop laughing cause I was really high man, been smokin' some real fine reefer so the man says, 'Suppose I break your head; that be funny, junkie?' 'Officer,' I says, 'I ain't no junkie. Take a look, man. You don't see any tracks, so why you callin' me names when I'm not doin' nothin' to you?' That's what I said, and he just jabs me in the side with his stick, like this, and he says, 'Next time I catch your junkie ass on my beat I'm gonna go up side your junkie head, you hear?' That's what he says man, those were his exacto words. But listen, I'm goin' up to Harlem tomorrow, got a guy who wants to score some smack, and I was just wonderin' do you want anything, you need anything like that?"

"Sure, Zarro, score me a nickel bag, and I'll pay you later."

Puppy yawns, fixing his one good eye on Zarro.

"I told them I was clean. What they want from me always hassling my ass? Out in the Haight they leave you alone, man, but here I don't know what's really goin' down, you know. Want a toke, man?"

"No thanks, Zarro."

"Say, I heard they zapped Siobhan last week."

"Yeah. But it wasn't last week, Zarro. It was last winter. Welfare department was hassling her, threatening to cut her off if she didn't see a shrink, so she went up to Bellevue and walked through the door marked **INPATIENT** instead of the one marked **OUTPATIENT**. They asked her a couple of questions, then decided to hold her for 'observation and evaluation.'"

"The wrong door?" Zarro laughs, kissing his python on the nose. "Man, how'd that happen?"

"She went to Bellevue to talk to a shrink. And once she was inside, they just wouldn't let her out."

"You've been in Bellevue, man?"

"No, but lots of places like it."

"Oh fuck yes. Me too. Hasn't everybody? Last time they locked my ass up half my friends were there. We had a little reunion. Got high, partied, screwed a lot when the orderlies weren't lookin', which was all the time cause one of my friends had lots a bread. Crossed the zookeepers' palms and made them deaf, dumb, and blind, man. But damn, man, wrong door, that's a gas."

"Ever been in there?"

"No man, like I say, not the big B. Heard too many fuckin' horror stories about that place and, man, you know what these old Polish fuckers say, 'Don't let nobody take me to Bellevue, cause I don't wanna come back in no coffin.'"

"Siobhan says giant rats run through the ward at night when the lights are off. She could see their shadows, and hear their claws skittering across the floor. The rats in her tenement are small compared to the ones in Bellevue."

"Yeah, man. Them rats probably feed on the patients, that's why. Better snack food up there. All they got to eat down here is junkies and hippies and Puerto Ricans. But up in Bellevue, man, like you know the hospital keeps them rats in cages. Feeds them little baby cats, and some day when they're really huge man, like kangeroos, they're gonna let them loose in the streets, and they'll come runnin' through the park, huge ugly fuckers grabbin' babies out of their cribs, scarfing up old ladies, suckin' the blood outa cops. Yeah, man, we could train them kangeroo rats to eat the man. Slurp. Two bites and the men in blue ain't nothin' but a pile a bones. Ha Ha Ha. Bellevue, man. Yeah, I heard stories. Who hasn't? Knew a guy was droppin' so much acid his eyeballs turned inside out. That ain't no lie man. Tripped one day and his eyeballs just spun right around in their own fuckin' sockets. White marbles, man. His eyes turned into these veiny old blood-streaked marbles. Disappeared, man. Say he's in Bellevue right now. Rat food. Heard they ate his feet off just last week. Hands the week before that. So there he is, just a little stub. And the kangeroos are watchin' him. Sittin' by his bed, man. Tongues out. Ears back. Waitin'. Watchin'. And he's thinkin' it's all just a bad trip, man. Just some bad shit he's soaked up with his tongue. That's how they keep us down. You know that. With kangeroo rats and cops and acid the government's fucked with so it turns our eyeballs inside out."

A policeman strolls by twirling his nightstick and Zarro closes his eyes until he passes.

"See what I mean, man. You see the way he looked at me. But it works man, it always works . . ."

"What works, Zarro?"

"If I close my eyes they freak."

"Really?"

"Yeah, man, I can become invisible any time I want. Like The Shadow, man. Remember: 'Who knows what evil lurks in the heart of man? Ha Ha Ha, The shadow knows. Ha ha ha.'"

"You grow up listening to the radio, Zarro?"

"Hell yes, didn't everybody?"

"I don't know. I did. Used to kneel on a little stool, in the kitchen, listening to the radio for hours and hours."

"So when the fuzz comes by I just become invisible man. I see him, but he don't see me, you dig? Fucks with their minds. Like presto, I'm here one minute, gone the next. Or maybe he's gonna reach for me, bust my head just for kicks. I press my magic twingger and I'm gone, man. Gone. Remember that one. The Buster Brown Show. Midnight the cat. Froggie the Gremlin. And Buster Brown says, 'Press your magic twingger Froggie,' and just like that, poof de doof, the frog disappears."

Zarro dances in circles, sings:

"'Hey kids. The Buster Brown show is on the air. The Buster Brown Show is on the air. Arf Arf Arf. Hey kids, that's my dog, Tide. He lives in a shoe. I'm Buster Brown, and I live in there too.' Yeah, man, dogs livin' in shoes. The Shadow, The Fat Man, The Green Hornet, Batman, I dug all them shows. Usta fall asleep with my head on the radio. Say man, you know who I seen last week?"

"No."

"Ginsberg, man. No lie, man. Just walkin' down Second Avenue. Hand-in-hand with some tidbit I never seen around the neighborhood before. Allen Ginsberg. Wow. You ever meet him?"

"No, never have."

"But you dig him?"

"I used to recite *Howl* to the nurses when I was in the snakepit, Zarro."

"*Howl,* man." Zarro lays his invisible guitar aside and adjusts his python as though it were a tie.

> *I saw the best minds of my generation destroyed by*
> *madness, starving hysterical naked,*
> *dragging themselves through the negro streets at*
> *dawn looking for an angry fix.*

"Oh man," Zarro laughs, "I scribbled that inside my senior English book in high school back in 1962, man. And when my teacher called me in to recite, had to memorize two hundred lines of poetry to pass outa her class, I did my thing:

> *Out out brief candle, life is but a walking shadow*
> *Who cowered in unshaven rooms in underwear, burning*
> *their money in wastebaskets and listening to*
> *A poor player who struts and frets his stuff*
> *with dreams, with drugs, with waking nightmares,*
> *alcohol and cocks and endless balls . . .*
> *A tale told by an idiot, full of sound and fury, signifying*
> *who got busted in their pubic beards returnin*
> *through Laredo with a belt of marijuana for New*
> *York.*

"She freaked out, man. Kicked me right out of class for using 'profanity'. I told her, I said, 'Listen Mrs. Kerensky. Ginsberg is the Shakespeare of our time. There's no difference between the two, just one uses 'fuck' and the other doesn't, that's all.' She didn't buy it man. Got Ginsberg banned from school altogether. Anyone caught carrying a copy of *Howl* went straight into detention. Schools and prisons, man, the same people runnin' them. Course it wasn't no big problem since only two or three of us wanted to be beatniks. The rest just wanted to get into college or the Marines.

"Yeah, man . . ." Zarro sucks smoke into his lungs. "Oh yeah, what was I sayin'? That chick I saw you with the other day, oh yeah, like she is fine man, very fine. Cunt like a fist. Mouth like a cunt. Oh," he starts to dance again, "oh yeah, I wouldn't mind ballin' her myself sometime."

"She's not my wife, Zarro. Her name is Beryl Cranshaw. Beryl, man."

Zarro giggles, strums his guitar a few times, coughs and spits. Puppy waits for the snake to make a move.

"Not my wife," Zarro shouts, pointing at me. "Not my wife. Yeah, like who's got a wife? You know anybody with a wife? You know any wives? Ever had one? I never had one. My old man did, but she split. I'd like to see a wife. Really. I mean. Wife? Wife. Listen to that poetry man. Listen to that. Poetry. I write poetry. Wife poetry. Wife and strive. How's that? How's that sound to you. You dig it? I do. Wife and strife had a life. O.K.? Wife and life had a strife. Oh. Wifeymouse. Wife in my house. Eating cheese. Please cheese on her knees if you please my wife. Ah man, Ginsberg's got nothing on me. I'm a genius. Zarro's got a wife. Right here man," pointing between his legs. "That's my wife. Nice nice wife suck my strife if you have a life I'll ball your little wife."

"You're a poet, Zarro."

"Yeah man, catch you later. I got to split. Stand still too long they start knowin' where you're at. *They're* down here man. On every one of these badass streets. But," he said, laughing, "don't matter if nobody else sees them, cause I do. I see *them*. Clear as day man. I know the game. Same game. Game same. Play same. I frame. You know the dame. Lame. Game lame. Gotta be, later man. Later for their secret agent bullshit. Want to spy you die don't cry cause that's why if you spy someday you gonna die lookin' in my window make your wife a wid-dow seein' down my scope take away your hope nope dope tie you up in rope take you to the river and cut out your liver so stay away don't play with my . . . MIND . . ."

"Later, Zarro."

Zarro adjusts his cape, bows to the babushkas and walks backward toward Avenue A, stopping every few paces to strum his invisible guitar and shout:

> *who howled on their knees in the subway and were*
> *dragged off the roof waving genitals and manuscripts*

The babushkas shake their heads in disgust. On their dining room tables, squeezed between snapshots of their grandchildren and portraits of Pope Paul are gold-rimmed photographs of their dead President, his smile charmingly coy and his eyes twinkling with mischief, as though he were going to share some anecdote about the tough Ukrainian coal miner who thought no baby-faced Harvard boy would ever make him, Nikita Sergeyevich Khrushchev, blink. The babushkas spray Windex on the glass, but their Camelot is dead and the streets are filling up with ragtag creatures with names like Zarro and Starlight and Groovey and Twinkle, and the park reeks of hashish and marijuana and un-washed bodies.

No one had talked on that long, cold, November subway ride, no papers even rustled, no one opened books. I stood on the platform at 51st Street with hundreds of other New Yorkers, listening to the train grinding its way in from Queens and the doors sliding open, and we boarded knee-to-knee elbow-to-elbow without a word, no words. In one corner of the train a construction worker in tan coveralls, hammer hanging from his tool belt, pressed his hands still gritty from work hard against his eyes. Tears ran over his knuckles, streaking through the dirt as he swayed with the train, sobbing into his fists.

The train made its usual noises, screeching around corners, brakes burning, slamming from side to side, but we were traveling in slow motion, or backwards. Doors opening and closing, the stations like giant crypts, silent, forboding. I picked up a copy of the Daily News. KENNEDY ASSASSINATED. PRESIDENT DEAD. LBJ SWORN IN. I walked to Siobhan's apartment. She was cooking fish-head stew, and when I showed her the paper she turned off the gas, pulled back the patchwork quilt on her mattress and slid beneath the covers. I poured a glass of whiskey, drank it, poured another and crawled in beside her. She smelled like fish and roasting chestnuts and when she wrapped her legs around me I wanted to crawl deep inside her, to be a tiny little cluster of cells floating warm and peaceful in a water bubble, without slumlords, junkies, and pushers, without cops or psychiatrists or mental hospitals or people who shoot dogs or other human beings just for sport, no shadows to chase, just floating in a timeless universe, and Siobhan and I stayed inside her apartment, sleeping and making love; I drank more whiskey and licked tears from her cheekbones and wondered why we were crying because the President resided on Olympus, rich, powerful, and untouchable. The President lived in a mansion and we slept in a tenement that smelled like pot and piss and stale cabbage and beer-vomit; he dined with queens and kings while we ate at the Catholic Worker with winos and people who'd been dumped from the welfare roles and people who'd been lobotomized by poverty. We seemed to live in the same country that Presidents lived in, yet we could never enter their world, they would never know anything about ours. And if I had been offered the choice between meeting Camelot, or eating a steaming plate of stuffed cabbage at one of the Polish restaurants on Avenue A, I was simply too hungry to pass up the food.

Siobhan and I wrapped together whispering and crying and wondering and waiting, and later I sat in a bar, watching JFK's funeral and listening to the mournful music, and the President's two-year-old son saluted and lines of weeping people passed by the flag-draped casket in the Capitol's rotunda. Jack Ruby shot Lee Harvey Oswald and the President's son saluted and I didn't go back to work and was soon out of money. When Siobhan kicked me out I was so drunk on Thunderbird wine that I tossed my suitcase—all my belongings—into Second Avenue, laughing when a cab smashed it to pieces. Later, I sat in the park, broke and homeless, trying to think where I would sleep that night and wondering why people kill presidents, and what it must be like to grow up rich and powerful like JFK.

I went further down, panhandling, stealing, lying to get money for alcohol, waking sick, hands shaking, in strange places, junkies snoring in the bathtub, light filtering through a set of ragged curtains, dusting rows of sleeping faces, weak sighs, doors slamming, water running, singing, tapdancing on the stairs, not knowing where I was or how I got here, only that I'd become so very adept at weaving spells. I could be a poet, school teacher, soldier, farmer, novelist, concert pianist, whatever persona the night demanded, whatever role procured another round of drinks. Smoke wrapping its legs around the White Horse Tavern's lights, Old Reliable's juke-box undulating, beer splashing over the 9th Circle's bar, and for a few hours my companion and I would sail across fantastic seas, exchanging lies the way we once swapped marbles in the schoolyard.

Cheap liquor is my shepherd, I shall not want.
My shot glass runneth over.
I will lie down in drunken pastures.
Yea, though I walk through the valley of blackouts
   I will fear no evil.
Last call. Amen.

About a year after JFK died, I was drinking in Stanley's when the bartender handed me the phone, grinning as though I'd won the Irish sweepstakes.

"Help me. Get me out of here," Siobhan begged.

"Where are you?"

"I'm in Bellevue. They locked me up."

"Who locked you up Siobhan?"

"The shrinks. I meant to go in the OUT door, but walked in the one marked IN by mistake. Now they won't let me go. Call my sister. Please. Tell her to get ahold of Dr. Simpson. He's the one I went to see that one time. They're going to send me to an upstate mental institution. Send me back. I won't go. I can't. They'll give me more shock treatments. Kill me."

Siobhan's sister promised to contact Dr. Simpson and, after drinking for several more hours, I started the long walk to Bellevue, past bodegas with green bananas, puny little chickens, and LOVE potions in their windows; past dingy bars where young enforcers stood around all day, combing their greasy hair, tapping their pointy shoes, waiting to find out whose kneecaps they were going to break, past rows of shops selling imitation watches, imitation suits, shoes, pants, underwear, imitation happiness; crossing 14th Street and heading updown, steam pouring out of grates, newspapers flapping along First Avenue like wounded birds, the wind chewing holes in my face.

I stood across the street from Bellevue Hospital, palms

sweating, heart pounding, only half drunk, dizzy with fear, my head shouting courage, my heart warning me to flee before the iron hand reached out, dragging me before the Inquisition where sentence would be passed before I could explain that I was there to visit a beatnik who opened the wrong door, didn't read the signs, didn't follow directions, just walked in and said the wrong thing to the wrong person because she, Siobhan, is a veritable Miss Magoo, walking barefoot and dreamy-eyed across busy streets while cabbies honk and curse and flick her the bird; a spaced-out Peter Pan who can't distinguish between a junkie and an oak tree because she lives in another galaxy, because her synapses are connected to a universe the Rorschach and MMPI and all the other "measures of mental well-being" are not designed to recognize and because Siobhan is the mirror into which, should the test-givers ever garner the courage to look, they might see themselves . . .

I stood there, shaking inside and out, the voice of reason and compassion urging me to walk across the street, directing me to enter an elevator, ring a buzzer, ignore the men in blue with their clubs and guns and faces set in a permanent death-head grimace. Just walk on by the past, directly by my fears, right onto the ward where giant rats run at night and the inmates' screams shatter dishes all the way to Brooklyn.

I wanted to turn downtown, tracing my steps to the safety of the streets where I had learned to trick fate and come up alive every morning, back to the familiar smell of people not making it, to the comfort of bodies in doorways, sirens and explosions, the fear that keeps pumping whiskey and adrenalin through my veins, sounds and sights familiar to me as the odor of amphetamine sweat in Siobhan's 6th Street nest.

I stood outside the hospital, composing diatribes and hating myself for not having the courage to go in, hating Siobhan for being stupid enough to trust any psychiatrist, even those behind the "IN" patient door. And then slowly, like a man who eats his last meal and is resigned to the gas chamber, I crossed the street and took the elevator to Siobhan's ward and sat down on a metal chair, facing her, and she wept and buzzers went off, people screamed, things crashed, the cops stood sentry outside.

"I'm scared," Siobhan said.

"It'll be fine," I assured her.

"But, they're gonna send me upstate. They said so."

"Why?"

"They won't say. Observation and Evaluation."

"Fuck that, Siobhan. Fuck them."

"Don't start trouble. That won't help."

"I won't, but I'm scared too. I hate it in here."

"The rats are really huge. They run at night. You can see their shadows. They look like horses. Hungry horses. I can't sleep. Too much screaming. The orderlies scream all the time."

Siobhan spoke in little gulps, coughing out a phrase, sobbing, coughing, sobbing. We held hands, trying to find a way out of Bellevue, but she was on welfare, and I was a bum. We didn't know any lawyers, and we were ex-mental patients, no one would listen to us. We would spend our lives lying to friends, neighbors, lovers, fellow workers, frightened that in the middle of our most scintillating lesson the school principal would rush into the classroom, demanding that we explain our demented past, wondering if, on the verge of getting tenure, the Dean would send an envoy, urging us to reconsider, demanding that we "get help," warning us not to disgrace the institution. We carried these fears, they carried us.

I walked to the end of the ward, and out. Siobhan waved, and I passed armed guards, careful not to appear to be watching them, trying hard to imagine them making love to their wives, hugging or reading bedtime stories to their children. Perhaps if we could just have a few drinks together we might tell stories, talk about our lives, discover just how much we have in common—that we are afraid to die, but don't really know how to live, that we need love, but don't know what it is, that . . . What really separates us? They were hired to guard these halls, but from what? Why didn't they just open the doors and let everyone run into the streets? Why not? The streets *are* Bellevue. Wild, loud, tempestuous, mad. So why not open the fucking doors?

I stared at their guns, the clubs, and the handcuffs attached to their belts. Their asses sagged, their eyes were shot with blood, and I feared and hated them so much that when one got shot I cheered, felt happy, laughed. I had seen the cops beat up old winos on the Bowery, seen them taking payoffs, seen them swilling whiskey in their squad cars, and I said nothing because the consequences of protesting, a savage beating and arrest, just weren't worth it. I watched, bowed my head, walked away.

I walked quickly toward the elevator, head down, trying to remember the magic words Zarro used to become invisible. The cage rattled downward and by the time I reached the sidewalk I was soaking in sweat, my stomach was in my knees, I felt dizzy, and lost. I had not been taken to Bellevue in handcuffs. I had walked in and walked out, strangely giddy, as though I survived a car crash in which everyone else died. I felt like singing. Not because Siobhan was in Bellevue, but because I wasn't.

The sun licks my shoulders, caresses my thighs. I doze with Puppy's head on my lap, and when I awaken, a man wearing only a pair of ragged red sneakers is sitting next to me on the bench, reading *The Daily News*. He turns the pages slowly, casually, as though relaxing, quite naked, in a lawn chair in his own back yard.

LBJ praises government in South Vietnam
Warns Communists not to widen war

Heat swirls from the sidewalk. Puppy's tongue stretches and drips. I wonder where Zarro goes at night, where he finds a nest. Like so many people who wander in and out of Tompkins Square Park, he seems more apparition than real. When he stands in front of me, strumming his invisible guitar and reciting *Howl*, I'm convinced he's real, but a few moments later he blips away, like a mirage. Puppy stretches, yawns, glances disdainfully about the park, and strolls toward Avenue C.

Beryl opens the door, naked except for a long white apron with "HOME SWEET HOME" stitched across the chest. Puppy leaps forward, licking her face and nearly knocking her down.

"Where've you been luv?" Beryl asks, turning to go back into the kitchen.

"Just hanging out in the park, talking to Zarro."

"That bloody little junkie."

"He was reciting *Howl* to the babushkas."

"And?"

"A little Shakespeare thrown in."

"Rubbish. What does Zarro know about Shakespeare?"

"I don't know, Beryl."

"Americans have no grasp of Shakespeare."

"Why not?"

"Because you're stupid, that's why."

"All Americans are stupid, Beryl?"

"Not all, just most."

When Beryl was eighteen years old, the happily married director who made her pregnant pleaded with Beryl to be his mink-coated concubine, a diamond-collared pussycat basking in some lovely Kensington window. She declined the offer. Her parents demanded the scoundrel's name. She refused to give it, and they exiled her to North America, where she gave the baby up for adoption, met a beat poet in Toronto, got raped by a man posing as a vacuum cleaner salesman, and nearly bled to death when the poet used a soup ladel to abort the six-week-old fetus she was carrying. The poet split for San Francisco, leaving Beryl destitute, and depressed enough to follow him to North Beach, where she worked as a copy writer to support her lover who smoked hash and wrote things like (Beryl kept scraps of his work):

> *Zombies riding through my mind*
> *Trying to find some deeper pass*
> *To the insanity of my dark prick*
> *Treating me like a useless spic.*

More fights, more poverty, ten thousand more quarts of Lucky Lager, ten thousand more gallons of cheap rose, a thousand joints, football-size chunks of hashish, tabs of acid, sprinkles of speed, and dear Beryl growing older but hardly less beautiful than early photos of her swaggering outside

Hampton Court, arm-in-arm with the mysterious, never-named (his head was snipped from the photo) director.

"Says he's going up to Harlem to score."

"My arsh. He's never been near bloody Harlem. Lives off his trust fund I'll venture, that phony. Like most hippies. They put on their costumes and take the train in from Long Island or Connecticut, walk around looking stoned, then go back home. This neighborhood was better off before they ever appeared. Now we've got the Mafia trying to buy up all the bars, pushers by the dozen, the uptown crowd coming downtown to peer at us like we're Llamas or something, the peelers meaner than ever, and the bloody landlords raising everybody's rent because the stupid realtors decided to name the Lower East Side 'The East Village.' My arsh. What bloody 'village'? This look like a village to you? Hastings on the Thames? Stratford on Avon, maybe?"

I watch her walk, the extraordinary tilt of her buttocks rising and falling, a racehorse trotting through a lovely summer dawn, her back muscular and tapering soapstone smooth, her thick curly blond hair trellising over her bare shoulders, her ballet dancer's legs trim-strong, long enough to wrap around the moon, the slight wet glint of silky, golden pubic hair, and something moving deep behind my scrotum, some weakness, knees buckling, slightly squeezing under-wear and Beryl stirring the soup, bent over apron falling tangled jeans and socks and shirt knees bending into her thighs and she reaching back with her thumb and forefinger gently squeezing sliding me in and out gripping the counter with one hand and me with the other, no curtains, our shadows pumping across one wall Beryl crying and we crumple to the floor among dead roaches, yesterday's *Sunday Times,* bottles of Guinness Stout, riding her down teeth in her shoulder clinging to her hair and she is pounding her forehead on the floor still sobbing through the crests of her orgasm.

"I'm cooking chicken soup. It's almost ready," Beryl sighs, kissing and licking me dry. Then, "Where have you really been all morning?"

"Just hanging out in the park with Puppy. Watching the babushskas watch the freaks. There's thousands of new people every day. Mostly day-trippers and bird-watchers from

Washington Square or uptown, hoping to get laid or to score drugs. Zarro had a snake wrapped around his neck."

"Yeah," Beryl whispers.

"Said the cops beat him up again."

"Oh."

"Made him roll up his sleeves, looking for tracks."

"Ummmmm."

"I think he's shootin' smack again."

"Amazing, I can't believe you could do it again so soon," lightly grazing me with her hand, then taking firmer hold, dreamily stroking while I continue talking even as the soup boils over the stove and the skin is burning off my knees against the hardwood floor and someone is pounding on the door but it's only the landlord demanding last month's rent, or the electric company coming to shut off the power, or the bodega we owe money to, or one of the people Beryl's conned so we can keep our little nest, and Beryl moaning again, the landlord with his ear to the door, coming in his fantasy, but the chainlock and deadbolt and police lock are secure and we fall asleep still locked together with the blinds open and the sun painting our naked bodies afternoon pastels. I dream that I'm going back to Iowa for the first time in four years and Billy Hicks is standing in my front yard wearing a black suit, and Frog Lady, Sissy, Dr. M, and Day Nurse, all dressed in black, are there to greet me and I am laughing and smiling and hugging them, but then I notice that on the lot where my parents' house once sat is a row of white wooden crosses, each cross bearing the name of someone in my family, and I begin to sob and curse and accuse Billy Hicks of killing my kin and he just grins and points to the far end of the lot where a tall white cross, set aside from the others, bears my own name, and then I awaken, as I have so many times before, whimpering and grinding my teeth.

Beryl is whispering "baby baby baby don't cry . . . I'm here . . . I love you . . ." and Puppy is standing over me, head tilted to one side, his good eye open wide, his pointed ears cocked as though he had been listening to my dream, waiting patiently, like some dog-therapist, to help me through its meaning.

Arriving at the Snakepit, Christmas '62

I remember this: Billy Hicks, the alcoholic who sat in the back seat of the squad car with me, hands cuffed like mine behind his back, shaking my hand and promising to see me again soon. Then a sleepy-eyed man (Hicks later told me that the man was a trustee from the state prison) demanding that I remove my clothes. A tiny bathtub filled with tepid water, the man handing me some green soap, leaving, locking the door, the water turning cold, steam turning to ice crystals on the windows, laughter outside, my knees knocking, skin turning blue, laughter, kneebends, pushups, jogging in place, jackhammer teeth and the man returning, not at all surprised to find a naked jogger in his office. "Bend and spread your cheeks," and his touching me lightly, carefully and with a motion so swift and efficient I had no time to react, forcing me cursing to my knees, tears of rage and humiliation beginning and quickly ending. "Guess you don't have no weapons or dope up there."

The man handing me a pair of light green trousers too big at the waist and too short in the legs, a green shirt with a number stenciled above the right pocket, and a pair of huge black clodhopper boots that flopped when I walked. The barber's sourdough breath and palsied hands as he shaved my head clean as a grapefruit, tufts of hair falling among squashed cigarette butts and bubblegum wrappers. Next, a visit to the dentist, who ground away at several teeth without administering novocaine. And then a long walk through a series of tunnels that connected the hospital's buildings, past blind Mary strapped to her chair and howling, naked four-year-old Jimmy running in circles and screaming "KISS ME KISS ME KISS ME," a kind of storage room where elderly men and women were crawling about like spilled worms. I held my trousers up, thumping in my huge black shoes on the way to quarantine, a small room with a cot where I lay in a heavily drugged stupor until Christmas morning.

CHAPTER 4

Thanks be to Giving

Eight or ten guests are sitting on crates and wobbly chairs, waiting for dinner to be served on the table I carried home from Avenue D, nailed back together, and covered with a beer-stained sheet. Anthony is a very old, very homely, bookseller. His nose is a huge sweet potato, he has elephantine, hair-sprouting ears, tiny pigeon eyes, and rotten teeth. He collects rare books and young men, and right now he's telling a story about the poet Hart Crane, claiming that he knew Crane well before the poet committed suicide by jumping from a ship into the Caribbean sea. One night, says Anthony, Crane was exhausted from working on his epic poem *The Bridge.* Out he went for a stroll, the streets dark, nearly deserted, no moon. Crane wandered about until he came upon a man standing in the doorway of an abandoned factory. They chatted briefly and returned to the poet's apartment, where the man insisted that they make love in the dark, talk in the dark, even eat dinner in the dark. Morning and sunlight scattered through the blinds, waking Crane who stretched, visited the bathroom, looked over his notes from the previous day's work and returned to the bedroom, where, says Anthony, lowering his voice for effect, he found that some horrible disease had eaten away his lover's fingers and toes; where, says Anthony, lingering on the horror of it all,

Crane found that the man he had caressed and kissed and had sex with was suffering from the ravages of leprosy.

"Oh my God," Alfie moans. "You're making that up, Tony."

"No," Anthony grins, stroking the beautiful young painter he's brought to dinner. "I knew Hart Crane rather well, and he told me this story himself."

"Repulsive," sighs the painter.

"Well," Alfie giggles, "rather different, that's for sure. One thing I haven't tried, yet."

"Did he get it?" asks a black poet who recently returned from twelve months on a Georgia chain gang.

"Get it?" Anthony winks. "Of course he got it."

"I don't mean sex," the poet complains. "I mean leprosy. Did he catch it?"

"I don't think so," Anthony says. "But he jumped off the ship a short time later, so perhaps he had no time to recognize the symptoms."

"Does it effect your . . . well, you know," a shy musician asks.

"No," Anthony assures him. "You can still, shall we say, function, even with your toes and fingers gone. For some reason, it leaves the most important parts of the human anatomy . . . intact."

In a gesture of magnanimity, our landlord hasn't turned the heat off for two whole weeks and Beryl, hoping to store warmth in the walls, cranks the thermostat up to ninety-five. Her thin white cotton dress clings wet-with-sweat to her breasts and hips as she rushes to and fro, bringing more wine, more Guinness, a fifth of gin, more marijuana, bending low over the table, no underwear, dancing in and out of the kitchen, no one taking any notice.

"Did you ever have sex with him?" Alfie asks.

"Who?" Anthony demures.

"Oh don't be cute, Tony. Hart Crane. Did you ever sleep with him?"

"Why do you ask?" Anthony sighs, blushing, his potato nose blinking on and off.

"When I was in Georgia," the black poet says, "they had the death penalty for sodomy."

"Well," says Alfie's dinner guest, a rather pale young novelist from uptown, "you're still walking around, aren't you?"

"That's not funny, Judy. For God's sake. I was arrested just for driving through that God-forsaken state. Got stopped by the sheriff in some twittly little town. Accused me of speeding. My license was expired so he threw me in jail. Then he decided I was cruising."

"Well weren't you?"

"I told you, no. I was on my way to visit my mother in Miami, that's all."

"And you didn't take a little detour?" Alfie teases.

"Alfie, you know how horrible that was," the painter pleads. "In those swamps with all those snakes and bugs and the sun and . . . it was beastly. Just for driving through, that's all. Don't ever drive through Georgia."

"Oh, don't worry, honey," Alfie giggles. "One thing I don't care for is reptiles, human or otherwise."

"Why did Hart Crane do it?" a beatnik poet asks.

"Sleep with the leper?"

"No, jump off the boat."

"I don't really know," Anthony says.

"Was he depressed?"

"I suppose so. Isn't everybody?"

"Please, let's change the subject," says the black poet. "Let's talk about something happy, like sex."

"I had the biggest rat in my apartment the other day," says Alfie.

"They're coming out," one of the guests agrees.

"He was about fifty pounds."

"Once," says the poet, "when I was sitting on the stool in prison a rat popped right out of the water and bit me. Had to have twelve stitches."

"I know a woman who lives over on Avenue D," Beryl says, toking on the fat joint Alfie rolls, "who was nursing her baby one night. She put the little angel in her crib, snuggled down and then fell fast asleep. Later that night she felt something sticky on her nipple and, thinking that the baby had managed to creep into bed with her, she reached down to pat its head. But when she felt at her breast there it was, an enormous rodent with its lips around her tittie, sucking, nursing it was, taking the milk right out of her body."

"Up in Harlem," says another guest, "a baby was found eaten, completely gone, by rats. Just a few bones and a little hair, that's all that was left."

"Don't they carry the plague?" Alfie asks.

"No," Anthony replies, sipping from his glass of gin. "That was in the 13th Century, Alfie."

"But they still attack children."

"Not a bad idea," Anthony's companion laughs.

"Wait. What did the woman do when she found a rat sucking on her tit?"

"She didn't do anything," says Beryl. "She was afraid to move, so she just let him drink until he was full, and then he crawled away."

"Oh God, that's disgusting."

"Fucking landlords."

"Too cheap to get exterminators."

"What good would that do?"

"Well, some."

"Not much. The city's filled with them. They're everywhere. They live in the walls. In the cellars. In the pipes. In the sewers. In the subways. Everywhere."

"No, alligators live in the subways."

"In the sewers, not the subways."

"People live in the sewers."

"And in the subways too."

"People and rats. What's the difference."

Beryl's eyes are turning a dangerous off-lemon, and the skin around her nose is starting to contract, pulling cellophane tight. I observe these things, but can't stop her. She keeps drinking. Her dress is soaked in sweat, tight around her nipples, inching up her thighs. She wobbles into the kitchen to check the turkey. We finish the gin, open a gallon of cheap Gallo, pass around another joint.

"I know a man who had a pet rat," Alfie says.

"You can't make a rat into a pet."

"Yes you can. They're very smart. It's just that they have to keep eating all the time, otherwise their teeth will grow up through their brains. So he brought home chunks of wood, and the rat chewed on them until there was no more room in that apartment. None at all. Sawdust and shavings from floor to ceiling. I swear to you, that rat filled the place with his gnawing."

"Why didn't he just let it go?"

"He loved it."

"Loved a rat?"

"That's the city," Alfie giggles. "People love strange things."

"Too bad you can't eat them."

"Yeah, solve the problem of world hunger."

"Soldiers in World War I did eat rats," says Anthony. "And people in India eat them even now."

"God," Anthony's companion cries. "That's the most disgusting thing I've ever heard."

"A rat for Thanksgiving."

"Too small, you would have to cook several."

"Baked rat."

"Sauteed in Guinness."

"Marinated in gin."

"Might be good."

"Hell, what's a squirrel but a rat with a long tail? People eat them."

"I wouldn't."

"Never have."

"They're too cute."

"People eat people when they're hungry enough. Ever hear of Donner Pass?"

"Oh yes, of course, our pioneer fathers, eating one another on their way to California."

"Should have looked for rats."

"Rats don't live in the mountains."

"They like cities."

"They prefer New York."

"Rats and queers," Alfie laughs.

"Speak for yourself, Miss."

"I always do, always have, never denied it."

"What, being a rat."

"No, being queer."

"You would deny it if you lived in Georgia."

"I didn't deny it in Ohio," Alfie says.

"I did, in California," Anthony's friend says.

"So did I, in Minnesota."

"I wouldn't," Alfie insists.

"Maybe that's why you got kicked out."

"I didn't get kicked out, baby. I left, on my own free will."

"Does your mother know?"

"Yes."

"Your father."

"Yes."

"And they kicked you out, right?"

"No, they just couldn't quite accept my 'lifestyle'."

"Having sex with men is a 'lifestyle'?"

"I just did it, that's all," says Alfie.

"Yeah," says the black poet. "And if you just 'did it' in Georgia, they'd just do you in the electric chair."

Beryl is singing in the kitchen, another dangerous sign. When I offer to help she gives me a shove.

"Go back there and drink with your little faggot friends."

"You're drunk, Beryl."

"I'm not drunk," she laughs, pulling her dress over her head.

"Put it back on, Beryl."

"Why? Afraid one of our guests might attack me."

"No."

"Not bloody likely, is it?"

"Come on, Beryl, let's put the meal on the table. Everyone's getting hungry."

"Don't touch it. I've been cooking all day. It's mine. I'll do it."

"All right, but let me help you carry the turkey. It's heavy."

"No. I said keep your bloody hands off."

Beryl balances the turkey on one bare shoulder, swaying and catching her balance, moving forward, a buoy in rough waters, bouncing into one wall, burning her knee on the radiator, backing toward the window, backing, forward again, hitting the table and lunging, unconscious and still clinging to the turkey, to the floor.

Alfie and I scrape up the dressing, put a pillow under Beryl's head, cover her with a sheet, and place the turkey on the table. While Anthony carves, he tells about the time he

61

met Edith Piaf in Paris, and Sylvia Plath in London, and Dylan Thomas in Wales, and his new boyfriend passes round the copy of *The Bridge* that Hart Crane signed "To Anthony with all my respect," and we look at the book, touching it as though it has some power to bestow on us, and of course it does because we know that it was written in blood, not ink, and that the author lies somewhere on the bottom of the sea. Beryl snores beneath the table while we raise our glasses in toast after toast, giving thanks to Bacchus and Dionysus and people like Hart Crane who give the world something more than shopping centers and banks and army barracks and chain gangs and executions and we toast Anthony for bringing such good gin, and the painter for his taste in hashish, and Alfie for leaving Ohio, and the slumlord for not turning off the heat, he wants to see Beryl prancing about in her underwear, and Alfie raises his glass, "To the outcasts of rat's ass flats. Merry Turkey Day my strange little friends." We toast Beryl for cooking this grand dinner and for not falling into the street with the turkey and, my own silent toast, for passing out before she called our guests, or me, any names. "To Beryl," we shout, "goddess of East Sixth Street," swilling our booze and telling more stories about poets and painters and saxophone players and all kinds of people we love and find inspiring and would like to meet and Beryl doesn't even stir, and doesn't wake up until late the next morning, when she draws a steaming bath and soaks in the tub for nearly an hour, toking on a roach, reading *Passage to India,* sipping white wine and gnawing on the drumstick Alfie wrapped in newspaper and tied with a little red ribbon, leaving it beneath her pillow with a note; a present, he said, from the turkey fairy.

CHAPTER 5

Where Pushers and Poets Dance

We wanted it to be like the cafes where Hemingway and friends drank during the twenties, a place we would write about when we became famous. In the beginning our dream seemed possible, even if the East River wasn't the Seine, Avenue C was not the Boulevard St. Michel, and the Lower East Side couldn't be the Left Bank. We were expatriates in our own country, poor but charming and witty, and when we had money we drank Pernod, smoked pot and danced to the Temptations, Four Tops, Supremes, the Beatles. We wrote avant garde poetry, painted avant garde pictures, picked up other exiles and had avante garde sex. We took care of one another, but it didn't last.

"Well here we are," says Julie Trees, tying off with a piece of rubber tubing. "Charge of the lunatic brigade. Ours not to question why. Ours just shoot up, fuck a lot, and die."

I watch the needle entering her arm, her eyes slowly closing, the roll of her head as the amphetamine hits its mark, not knowing how prophetic her words will be—Mike spreading his wings in psychedelic flight. Richard's mind a psychedelic Humpty Dumpty that all his father's money couldn't put together again. Chris stabbed twice in the chest by the woman who wanted to kill me. Mary Catherine made pregnant by a pusher who coils in the Old Reliable Bar & Grill, a black bandanna wrapped round his refried head, flicking a six–inch stiletto at suburban hippies. Alfie, my friend, teacher, and lover, though he never ever touched me, so absurdly dead.

Ragged stretch marks criss-cross Julie's stomach and needle tracks run like rows of tiny insect bites along her emaciated forearms. A towering oaktree, its trunk anchored in her navel, climbs upward across her large acorn-tipped breasts.

"Never seen no tattoo like this one have you baby? But listen now, why don't you just try a little shot. Just once, that's all I'm askin'."

"No thanks."

"So drink your ass into an early grave, see if I care."

Blood shoots into the tube as she presses the plunger and the tree bends to a soft quiver, waving its branches, the trunk rising and falling, acorns swelling.

"Baby, you think too much," Julie whispers, untying the tube. "Your brain is hyperactive. One a these days it's gonna burn up, POOF. Smoke'll come outa your ears. You'll just be crispy fried Cowboy. Yeah, man, dig it," Julie laughs. "Crispy fried Cowboy, Peking style."

Hotwired, sweating and gesticulating, Julie paces the room, a bare bulb casting Rorschach visions on the walls—squid, pterodactyl, vampire bats, great white sharks. Sweat dripping from her forehead, running over the tree's limbs, collecting around the acorns, down her breasts.

"I shock you, don't I, baby? You don't really like to see a woman walking around naked, do you? Doesn't lady Beryl do that for you? Fuck her, man. Saw her in the park the other day with that spade cat that dresses up in all them costumes. Captain Hook, Roy Rogers, Superman, Marilyn Monroe, all that silly shit. Don't know who the fuck he thought he was that day, but Beryl's sittin' on his lap, lickin' his face like she's a mama cat washin' off one a her kitties. Listen, man, you're still clinging. Still holding on to all those fairy tales you done got fed in nursery school. Still wishin' you could be a baby again and mummy'd wrap you up in red, white and blue, tuck you into your duck duck crib with Poohbear and stuff a pacifier in your mouth."

The neon sign outside our window turns the leaves on her chest reddish green and a man sings in Spanish, loud and plaintive and way off-key. A child cries. A couple makes loud angry love. Inside the airshaft a radio squawks.

President Johnson said today that he intends to send 100,000 more troops to South Vietnam ... Martin Luther King plans to escalate his campaign of civil disobedience throughout the South ... J. Edgar Hoover says communists on the move in the United States ...

I tear up my mother's latest letter, sailing the tiny pieces into the street. Come home, she writes. Just a word, she implores, and a one-way ticket will be in your hand. Waking in some rotten crash pad, elephants stampeding through my head, my heart contracted into a fist of depression, I am tempted to accept. I imagine stepping off a Greyhound bus and the welcome home ride and later, after the traditional Sunday dinner, walking through the woods where I stormed dug-in Japanese soldiers and killed thousands of Germans in hand-to-hand combat, and a soft wind playing through the trees, the aroma of ripe apples, grapes heavy with juice, falling alseep to the melancholy hooting of a freight train heading for Chicago.

"See what I mean Cowboy," Julie Tree shouts. "Like you think you'll be lying in your coffin and everybody's standin' around cryin' cause they never understood you, didn't treat you nicer. A real old-fashioned wake, hordes of people just choking on remorse. And you're lookin' down from your heavenly perch, glad they're being punished for not treatin' you better."

About to die, wrote one of my sisters, mother said not to blame you, even though you did abandon her and your own father.

Dear Sister, I replied. Save your guilt for your own children. Feed it to them for breakfast. Heap it on their Cheerios. Butter their bread and brush their teeth with it. Shampoo their hair in it. Have your parish priest baptize them in it.

Fill up the bathtub and drown yourself in it. Weave a rope out of it and hang yourself. Stuff it into a shotgun shell and blow our your brains with it. Poison your husband's martinis with it. Exchange it for Xmas with your mother. Can it in pickle jars so you can eat it through the winter. Bake it, fry it, boil it, shoot up with it, anything you want, but leave me alone!

Recovered from her apparent heart attack, mother wrote to say that I'd broken my father's heart and I replied that his heart deserved to be broken, that the family name should disappear into the great cruel void of the universe, and that I intended to stay here, on these streets, for the rest of my life. And you are quite right, I added. I am a bum. Quite right, I am wasting my life. Quite right, I am an alcoholic. Quite correct, I am fucking every human being in New York, and a few dogs, cats, and horses as well. A good way to die.

"Forget all that nostalgic crap," says Julie. "We're alone. All alone, man. Why can't you dig it? Just you and the streets now. The sidewalk's your family, booze your sacrament, ballin' your afterlife. Get it through your head, man. Home's just a blank old tombstone. Ain't nothin' there. Not the date you were born, not the date you check outa here. We're fleas, man. And when doggie shakes we fly on to the next karma. Wow man, what fun.

"Listen to me, you little farmer. Ain't no goin' back to Des Moines, or anywhere else. Don't you know that yet? Look at you, you raggedy-assed motherfucker. No job. No home. No nothin' man. You're not a junkie, you don't shoot smack, oh big fuckin' deal. You're a wino, man. A bum. What people in this city call a stewbum, crumbum, scumbum, bum bum. Welcome to the bottom of the fucking bottom, baby."

In the street below someone is arguing over money. "You owe me fifty dollars, man. You owe me, goddamn it. Pay up you cheap motherfucker. You owe me fifty dollars, pay me before . . ." I wait for shots, sirens, the swish swish of a hose washing away the blood. Julie hands me a pint of Thunderbird wine.

"I mean how long you been in the streets now, man? But you just can't seem to dig it. No more Peter Pan in Greenwich. No more Mary Poppins in Scarsdale. No more Jesus walking on water in West Hampton. That show's over. They've done gone. Split. It's a new scene. This is it. This is where it's at. All we got now, baby."

A pair of pterodactyls are fighting on one wall, flapping their wings, dipping and diving for the kill, spinning one wing ripped off toward the water SPLASH and a shark rising as the monsterbird lands, grabbing the wounded creature in its jaws, heading for the bottom.

Julie and I drift through the Lower East Side with a network of junkies and winos, squatting in vacant apartments until Con Ed turns the gas and electric off and the cops come to kick us out. She disappears, only to turn up in one of the crash pads with a blanket and pillow, a battered saucepan, some soup or a can of beans, things we put together to create a small, ephemeral milieu in one squalid corner of the squatters' pad. We spread our blanket, place the pillow carefully in the middle and sit around a pot of beans, eating and talking and later making love as though the blanket is a real room with walls and windows and a bed.

"You want my life, cowboy. The truth, not some lame *True Confessions* story. I'll tell you what it's like in Respectableville. Just listen. And don't fall asleep when I talk. Not this time, you little fuckhead. When my stepfather was raping me he used to say, all the time he was doin' it, 'Isn't it fun? This is fun, isn't it Julie? You really like this, don't you baby?' And when it was over, when he'd shot his wad for the fourth time, he'd warn me that if I said anything he'd cut me up and put me down the garbage disposal. He'd say, 'Come on, Julie, make it fun, Julie. Pretend like I'm an ice cream cone, Julie. Vanilla fudge and it explodes in your mouth, Julie. Like I'm an ice cream cone gonna blow up, gonna hit the ceiling. Get ready, catch me, Julie. Open your mouth, catch your daddy's ice cream, Julie.'

"I ran away. Cops brought me back. Took off again. Brought me back. Sent me to a shrink. Put me on Thorazine. One night I told my stepfather that I was gonna wait for him to fall asleep, then cut off his balls with a carving knife. Snip them off and feed them to the beagle. But he was a churchgoer, lawyer, golf-playing upstanding righteous snake-tongued white blond-haired motherfucker. Dwight D. Eisenhower, George Patton, Richard Nixon, Pat fucking Boone all rolled into one. Slick. Smooth. Sly. A real fuckin' M . . . A . . . N . . . , cowboy. Split-level home, wife, kids, job, split-level brain, split level personality. Who the fuck would believe a punk kid like me anyway?"

Julie lays back on the bed, drained from her monologue, lighting a joint and sucking the smoke deep into her lungs. 1 tell her about the tiny pill on my plate that meant they would strap me down after breakfast and shoot me full of sodium amatyl so that my arms and legs wouldn't break when Dr. Hotchkiss ran electricity through my brain, and I told her about the elderly college professor who slipped with each electro-shock treatment deeper and deeper into senility, his afternoons spent playing solitary games of checkers, jumping and rejumping his own men, saliva dribbling from his unshaven chin, his hands palsied, voice a babble.

Before Dr. H. began treating the professor he was a fine story teller and a skilled player of board games. After the third treatment his memory began to fail. After the sixth, he stuttered monosyllables. By the ninth he was an imbecile, alone in one corner of the ward, past present and future welded into one endless solitary game of checkers. The treatments continued, for the professor, and for me.

I tell Julie that I'm afraid my family will track me down and extradite me to Clarion for more shock treatments, and that I'll wind up like the professor, my frontal lobes melted together and my brain a dead sea, drooling into my cereal, talking to the squirrels when the orderlies take me out for an afternoon walk.

"New York?" Julie laughs. "Who's gonna find you or anyone else here? Who cares? Place's just a lunatic asylum without a roof, Cowboy. No way to sort out the crazies from the sanies. But listen, Cowboy. Just think about it, man. A few years back we were drinkin' slow gin at the senior prom and puking our guts out while our boyfriends tried to figure how to snap our bras off in the backseat of their '56 Chevies. Oh man, Elvis Presley, James Dean, the Big Bopper, Milton Berle, Lucille Ball, Ricky Nelson. That's who we were. So what happened? Me, a cheerleader, on the swim team, the Dolphin Club, and even after they locked my ass up the first time I still wanted to be a good little girl, still wanted them to like me, even if they weren't capable of fucking loving me. Just look at us," waving at an imaginary photograph album. "Our long silly dresses, our pumps, our little pageboy haircuts, cut from the same cookie-cutter, all off the same fuckin' assembly line, but Jesus, I ain't lyin' I wanted to be one of those cookies. Once I did, Cowboy.

"We believed in the virgin Mary and coitus interruptus. Thought our little titties would get bigger if we massaged them every day. Thought we couldn't get knocked up if our boyfriends got their rocks off standing up. And even when we did do IT, we just closed our eyes and counted to ten, then rushed home to repeat a thousand Hail Marys to our teddy bears."

Julie spins out her monologue, poking her finger into my ribs when I start to doze, but the wine and the suffocating room drag me down and when I wake she is gone, and so is the twelve bucks I scraped together for a week at the Albert Hotel, where I planned to lie in bed for several days, drifting in and out of sleep, listening to the cacophony of drug deals and propositions, fierce arguments, and hallucinogenic monologues outside my door. Placing my hunting knife on top of the dresser at night, pushing the dresser against the door and shoving the bed up against the dresser. Then, filling the sink and soaking my socks and underwear, draining the water each time it turned black. An hour-long shower, wrapped naked in cool sheets, lying safe and clean and in-cognito—always giving the clerk a false name—knowing that when the week was up I would go back to the streets, broke and hungry, searching for another nest.

When I reappear after my fortnight-long outing with Julie Trees, Beryl weeps, calls me a faggot, and cracks me over the head with an empty Guinness bottle. We make silent fist-clenching love and later she says I can stay if I stop chasing other women, cut down on my drinking, and hold a job for more than a week. I accept her terms and the very next morning, so hung-over that the machine's keys melt before my eyes, I sit down to a typing test at Office Extras, passing it with ease, going on to the spelling and grammar:

**Explain what's wrong with the following sentence:
"Me and my brother ain't going to eat no more pie."**

The manager of the agency is a young and very beautiful
Jewish woman who laughs when she reads my application.

"There's a two-year gap here? Were you ... in the
military ... ?"

"Yes," looking sadly heroic, "I was in the Marines."

"Oh," she says, knowing I am lying. "Did you learn to type
in the Marines."

"Yes, ma'am I did."

"Do you think," she is wearing a low-cut summer dress
which I keep taking off, "that you can really hold a job?"

"Sure," trying to control my palsied hands—Beryl gave me
subway fare only, not even a little extra for a hotdog at Ned-
ick's, or a shot and a beer at the Blarney Stone.

Marlene is having difficulties, her hands shaking so hard
that she can barely fill in the little circles with her number 2
pencil. On the back of an envelope I compute that at $1.65
per hour I've made $4.85 so far that morning, before taxes.
Marlene dips toward the silver flask she keeps in her desk
drawer. Dip Dip, Sip Sip. Her eyes are a pale, rather foggy
green. She plucks her eyebrows, sketching them in again with
a charcoal pencil. Her eyelids are luminescent blue, her teeth
the color of grass gone too long without water. In the right
hand drawer of her desk, next to her flask, Marlene keeps a
mini-scrapbook of her acting career. Photos of an extraordi-
narily beautiful woman emerging from a limousine; posing
under a marquee with *Marlene C. Bridgewater* spelled out with
lightbulbs; being hugged by a very elegant man in front of
the Four Seasons. Pressed flowers, ticket stubs, newspaper
clippings, programs.

On opening night of her first show, says Marlene, the pro-
ducers sent a limousine to her apartment, and there was a
wonderful dinner at the Ritz. Her dressing room was literally
overflowing with flowers from well-wishers, and finally curtain calls and walking on stage, the lights blinding her at first
and the audience reciting each line as *she* spoke it, laughing
and clapping and even crying, her own lines coming directly

from God, yes God, and she was speaking not from her head, not even from her heart, but from her soul, each word hanging in the air like fairy crystals, like wonder, like truth and beauty and pure magic.

"Oh it was a *magic* evening all right," Marlene says, dipping to her silver flask and rising, cheeks glowing, eyes focused not on the coding and tabulating but on her audience, "I might even call it divine." Scratch scratch. Marlene removes a tube of lipstick from her purse and a small, gold-plated mirror, squinting into the mirror as though, within, she can actually see the past. She lights a cigarette, sucking the smoke deep into her lungs and delicately tapping the ashes into her left hand. All around us people are filling in little circles with number 2 pencils. *"Would you say that this ad is very exciting, moderately exciting, somewhat exciting, dull?"* I tabulate the responses. I would say this ad causes paralysis of the cerebellum, coronary arrest, instant brain damage.

Marlene recites a few lines, dips, watches the clock. "Oh, I could tell you all their names, all the stars I knew, the people who used to come by for brunch or cocktails, the ones who summered on the Cape when my husband, God bless his soul, was still alive and we were young and ever so golden. Brunches in the Hamptons, cocktails by roaring fires in Oyster Bay, walking on the beach, oh, yes, right out of *The Great Gatsby*. You wouldn't know Scott Fitzgerald's work. How could you, growing up in Idaho? No time, I should imagine, for things like art and the theatre. Well, after all," she said, dipping, "that was another era altogether. Another time, yes. When things were more, shall I say, elegant. When I . . ." but her voice trails off as she continues to mark her stack of sheets, crumpling every other one and tossing it into the wastebasket.

Marlene boards a cab at lunchtime, and doesn't return until the next morning. To help us through the afternoon, the company nurse distributes tiny tabs of speed and Alka-Seltzer, covers my poor blistered feet with salve, and orders me to trade my plastic shoes in for a pair of real ones. With what, I ask? Your good looks, she laughs. When the speed kicks in I mark, mark, mark, breaking the lead on a half dozen pencils, watching the hands on the clock move backward.

I ride the subway each morning in mid-July, wearing a borrowed suit made out of killer ants, a barbed-wire tie, and a pair of shoes that are grinding holes in my feet. Strap humping and sweating, soggy, wilted, herd shuffing off the IRT, dead eyes up the escalator, hands palsied from another night of heavy boozing and there to sit, rowing the galley from 9 to 5, sorting through stacks of computerized forms, coding and tabulating responses to moronic questions about shampoos that make men bald and deodorants that make women sterile and laundry soaps that will eat away the brains of our nation's children until, released from our chains, we plummet nose-to-nose in the late afternoon elevator. Nose to nose silence, eyes on the ceiling, eyes on the floor, eyes turned inside out and the doors sliding open, crowding us into a light rain, the wonderful aroma of wet sidewalk, sauerkraut and onions, chestnuts, the pounding of this frenetic city whose streets make my heart race with expectation, umbrellas popping open, papers held over heads, the race for home beginning.

Walking by St. Patrick's Cathedral, wishing I could go inside and pray, yet certain that if God exists He understands why I don't enter. When I was a boy my mother pointed to a stack of bricks just down the street from our home. Satan's chimney, she said, and he was down there, watching me, waiting for me, ready to pounce if I lied or cheated or stole. I loved God very much, and couldn't understand why He would allow the evil one to live so close to my parents' house (I held my breath and ran in terror whenever I passed the devil's chimney). When I got older I began to wonder why, if indeed human beings were made in God's image, our lord and master would want to keep a ledger of all his subjects' wicked thoughts and deeds. After all, I didn't create the first humans out of some primordial slime. God did. I didn't tempt Eve with an apple. The snake did. My sperm didn't fertilize Eve's egg. A man named Adam did that. I didn't even ask to be born, and I didn't find it very amusing that God created man in His image, then sat back and watched his own likeness starting wars, building concentration camps, becoming slumlords, prostitutes, cops, and drug dealers.

Limousines line up along 5lst Street, dark, sleek, and sinister. Now and then I catch a glimpse of someone, or some part of someone—a wrinkled, heavily jeweled hand, a face drooping with rouge and heavy earrings, a gargoyle's mouth—and I imagine the mouth moving, directing the driver to throw this long black machine into gear and race for home where Grace is cooking dinner and Toby is cleaning the stables and Marge is making the beds and Filipe is building a fire in the study and George is pouring a glass of Sherry and arranging a plate of cheese and crackers and the dogs will race down the U-shaped drive when they hear the limousine coming and the gargoyle will open a package of bones saved from lunch at the Top of the Sixes, tossing them out to the prancing animals while Sam pops an umbrella and opens the door to the soothing aromas of cherry wood and things simmering in white wine and fresh cut flowers and polished mahogany and later a demitasse of espresso by the fire.

I leave the subway at Cooper Union, thinking about the afternoon I saw W.H. Auden on the IRT, slippers on his feet and his pockets stuffed with mail. People were giving him the knee and elbow just as they would any other rider, and when he left the train I followed him for a while, wanting desperately to pay him homage but unable to even say hello. My literature professor in college worshiped Auden, telling us that he might not be a God, but he was far above ordinary mortals. Auden disappeared into some Third Avenue dive, and I kept walking, wishing I'd never seen the real man.

I walked along St. Mark's place to Second Avenue, passing the apartment where on Sunday afternoons a young woman removes her blouse and unsnaps her brassiere allowing her charming breasts to spring free and lightly quiver while she plays the cello for a group of rapt music-loving voyeurs and soon the police, who can hardly believe their lucky-day eyes, arrive to inform her that she is breaking some law by exposing her breasts, and she continues playing, and New York's finest place her under arrest, throwing a blanket over her torso and leading her past cheering fans to be fingerprinted and photographed and booked, it seems, for violating the city's code of decency.

On past the Le Metro Cafe, where Ed Saunders, publisher of *Fuck You* magazine, holds court with his coterie of "I write about having sex with you, you write about having sex with me" friends, ooooohing and awwwwing when someone recites a particularly erotic line. I've often paid the .25 cents to keep out of the cold, another dime for coffee, wishing I knew how to fill a cafe like this with oooohhhhhing and awwwwwing aficionados of fellatio terza rimas and cunnilingus haikus. When you fall asleep there, people assume you're meditating or communicating with the muse and leave you alone.

One night a young man with a four-hair goatee and peyote button eyes recited a poem about his girlfriend's throbbing pussy and his own totem pole thrusting in and out of her throbadob, and I was nodding into my own long empty cup when one of Siobhan's Bellevue pals strode to center stage, clutching a stack of wrinkled napkins, his eyes wolfing down the audience. He informed the crowd, in a squeak-opera voice, that the Le Metro Cafe was a pretty jiveass place, that everything he'd heard so far was repetitive, declassé, passé, derivative dogshit, but that in spite of his audience's stupidity and lack of creativity he intended to read one of his own poems, a really far-out work, he said, that had taken him many weeks to complete, finally honing it to perfection at just this historic moment, even while he was suffering through all that other boring, really uncool play de dippy day. He paused, face raised to the magic mushroom spotlight, drug-fried eyes rolling like dice, and then he started to shriek:

> *Do not go gentle into that good night,*
> *Rage rage against the dying of the light,*

Too stunned to react, the audience first stared, then glared at the young man who continued howling line after plagiarized line. A poet jumped to his feet, spilling his coffee over the manuscript he'd been working on, waving his arms, making a fist, shouting "Hey man, that's Dylan's poem, not yours. That belongs to Dylan Thomas. You didn't write that, you fuckin' phony." The young lunatic scanned the room, cornered, hurt, enraged. "Yes I did, man. I worked all fucking night on this poem, *all night* man, all day and night on this ONE motherfucking poem. You've never heard it before. It's MINE, man. I wrote it. I was inspired by Neptune to put it down. He came to me in a dream. An oracle ordered me to do it, man. So I did did did that's what I did."

He recited a few more lines.

"Liar."

"Give him the hook."

"Not cool, just not cool, man."

"No respect for Dylan's memory."

"Asshole."

"Someone please stop him."

Siobhan's friend continued reciting, even when a hand yanked him sideways by the collar and someone grabbed his hair and a chair tipped, a coffee cup broke, and he was pushed through the front door still squealing that none of the dippy dap dummyshit shats appreciated his work, everyone stole from him, took his titty tit torn be little nit born poems, put them in print and tried to pretend they were their very very own. "I wrote it, you faggots. I'm a poet just like you. I can write better poetry than any of you cocksuckers. You phonies. You steal my work. But the gods know, oh, yes, they do daddy foo coo coo, who writes these things. They know all right. And so," he paused at the door, smiling, closing his eyes, "does the man with the black book. Ha ha ha."

I pass the building where Siobhan had introduced me to a soon-to-be famous folk singer who was lying barefoot on a double bed—next to him, his wife and her lover playing touchy feely, smoking a joint and giggling, and his first album cover heralding this new troubadour of the streets, this boy who knew New York City sooooooo deep in his soul that he could wail its sadness, its violence, its down-and-out landscape that—according to the hype on the cover—the singer had tramped through and slept in and felt the sorrow right down to the bottoms of his blues singing feet.

"I don't remember seeing him drinking on the Bowery or eating in the missions or giving blood in the bloodbanks," I scoffed, after we left the singer's pad. "My ass. He knows as much about the streets as I do about opera. Soul of the city boy. Ought to be soul of chickenshit. Where's he work?"

"He doesn't. But so what, you don't either."

"Where's he get money?"

"Who cares?"

"I care. From his rich parents, that's where," I screamed, pumped up with Thunderbird, which contained some crazy-making drug.

"That's none of your business. He's a musician. He doesn't have to work."

"Yeah, like all the poser punks around here. Pretending they live in the streets, so down and out, so desperate and when you walk into their pads, what do you see, Siobhan? Stereos, good food, good pot, a television set, and when they get tired of parading through the park they go home to Long Island and mommy rubs their backs and daddy gives them more money and they come back here all ragged and down and out again. Fuck that, fuck them, fuck your singer . . ."

"Stop it," Siobhan begged.

I took a drunken swing at her, missed and stumbled sideways raising my right hand to catch the piece of glass she swung at my neck, slashing a two-inch gash to the knuckle bone, and we walked to St. Vincent's hospital and sat in the emergency room, blood spat spatting onto the floor, and I imagined I had been there—I'd heard the story so many times before—the night Dylan Thomas was carried in from the White Horse Tavern where he'd been pounding down a sea of shots that finally stopped his great Welsh singing. I loved listening to him recite his work, especially *A Child's Christmas In Wales*, and I sat bleeding and wondering about the mystery of his gift and why this chubby man, swollen from drink, had been chosen to sing the beauty of the sea and the strange ebullient torment of living and loving and dying, and "Thank you, again, Mr. Thomas," I said aloud.

After he died, Dylan's wife wrote that St. Vincent's staff didn't know a scalpel from a soap spoon or something like that, and I waited for hours among fellow drunks who were bleeding, babbling, vomiting, smelling up the world, waiting to be patched up one more time and sent back to the Bowery, an intern finally taking my hand, thick now with coagulated blood, and scrubbing it with a huge wire brush as though it were a hambone needing trimming while great salty tears of remorse ran down my cheeks and the intern poured rubbing alcohol into the wound and wrapped it round with gauze and tape, Siobhan insisting that she didn't really want to kill me, just wanted me to calm down, and we walked through Washington Square Park and across the Bowery and I held my great puffy white boxing glove aloft as we made love on her life raft in her squalid, but warm, little nest.

I walk south on Second Avenue, passing the La Mama theatre, where a young playwright named Sam Shepard produces his avant garde plays, and where my friends and I read our own poetry to small but enthusiastic audiences who are hoping to hear, or perhaps discover, a reincarnated Rimbaud, Verlaine, Wilde, Baudelaire, or Apollinaire. Before reading, I drink myself into a stupor in some den of loneliness on Second Avenue where the bartender speaks in monosyllables, the patrons have all been dead since 1956, and the alcohol smells and tastes like my high school locker room. I sit there, waiting for some vision to strike, for the muse to rise from the jar of pickled sausages and carry me, directly, to the front cover of *Poetry* or the *New Yorker,* for the rotgut to burn away all lingering inhibitions, springing loose the subconscious, spinning masterpieces across the napkins on which I scribble with a ballpoint pen, but it doesn't matter if the critics fail to show at our readings as long as someone whispers egobursts into my ear and plays my body like a mandolin, assuring me the muse is mine for the asking, greatness merely a drunken evening or two away. I read poems like *The Man he was.*

> My father was an indian and he
> refused to take scalps
> *the lonely stretch of birds on highway*
> *wires*
> *can't be imitated, emulated, or later*
> *reproduced.*
> Sometimes he would tell me secrets:
> Holy wine is drunk by children
> taken together with leftover flesh.

He joined the army, became salvaged, and
solicited others for his salvage
forming a non-fighting, non-klling, heavy-
loving personnel, calling it
The Army of Salvation. And when
the bulk of trucks roll, men smile from
inside, do not stop,
the rope threads straight through justice
needle sprung down and out of life.
Often his men would play drums and
when the sun refused to look at justice
they would substitute a workingman's song.
Forward soldiers, forward on, we us I and
must go on, son, sonofabitch. It
was beautiful to watch. And even now I
think of him, standing on highways, kissing
windows, teaching songs, drinking with men
and forming armies.

Walking home now with empty pockets, stepping over bodies, the streets filled with garbage, disgusting heaps of dogshit
everywhere, and it is too early for Alfie to be behind the bar
at the Old Reliable and I can't get any credit at Stanley's
because the owner only gives it to a few of the stuffed beatniks he keeps round the place to draw in a crowd, but perhaps someone will recall my generosity and stand me a
charitable drink or two for I have squandered another day
of my life and the sickness goes deeper than bone, to the
place where nausea squats beside a pot of death, and the
psychiatrists were always demanding to know why I refused
to work, as though there is something intrinsically noble,
something universal, something archetypal, something like
God almighty, about slaving away so that someone else can
sail their yacht round and round our great big world, and I
would attempt to tell them about the hole in the pit of my
stomach that grew and grew when I stood on an assembly
line or whenever I spent eight hours shoveling sand or washing dishes or digging ditches or cleaning toilets—my first job
out of high school—or carrying huge canvas donkey bags
stuffed with papers through snow up to my waist at 5:00

a.m. so afraid that I kept my father's .38 revolver in my canvas bag and one morning the bushes trembled and I squeezed the trigger, the world exploding, a bullet missing my right foot by inches, blowing a huge black hole in the yellow bag, powder burns on my leg . . .

I tried to tell the inquisitors about W . . . O . . . R . . . K, and how the hole always grew bigger until it became me, me the hole, the hole that I felt was me, not bones and flesh and thoughts and feelings but just one expanding, nauseating hole that seemed to walk and talk through thick, impenetrable darkness, a molasses world where I swam gasping for breath and it got deeper with each hour, each dollar per hour, until I stood on my tippy toes begging for air and the boss coming down the line or over the rafters and in the door demanding to know why I was just standing there, why I had that strange decomposing look on my face and I would try to explain to him (I never had female bosses) that I was becoming a hole, a living, walking, talking, hole, and that I really wanted to be a human being not a HOLE but everyone kept insisting that in our family we became holes, in our neighborhood people became holes, in our church everyone agreed to be holes, in our state the governor was a hole, in our nation congresspeople were holes, our president was a hole, people who worked for a living were holes . . . holes put meat and potatoes on the table . . . holes put a roof over our heads . . . holes pay the bills that holes need to pay if they wish to continue being real HOLES.

And when I said I didn't want to be a hole because, deep down, beneath that place where it felt happy to be a hole, where it felt like belonging to be a hole, where it felt cuddly and all nicey nice to be a hole, and where I knew that being a hole was what I would have to be for the rest of my life, for eternity, for this karma, for this trip on this little snapfinger moment called life, that I just DIDN'T WANT TO BE A HOLE, they said I needed help to become a good hole again, that drugs and elecro-shock treatments and a few more weeks on some nut ward would make me want to be a hole again and I would agree to act like a hole and *be* whole again.

But it didn't work because I couldn't, no matter how hard I tried, be a good hole again and it didn't matter which hole told me to be a hole. I had lost something about being a hole, something necessary to be whole, and I would just have to figure out something new, something about not being a hole, something about being something that no one seemed to grasp the infinite possibilities of being, and that was NOT A GODDAMN HOLE.

Years later, ensconced on my favorite perch at the Old Reliable Bar & Grill, I ponder the miracle of alcohol—steady, salubrious, restorative, opening closed channels, soothing paranoia, blessing megalomania, combing its nimble fingers across the great gloomy waste of another pay little-by-the-long-boring-hour-day. The back room of the bar is jammed with hippies and beatniks, poets and painters, daytrippers and hustlers, pushers and killers, young quarterbacks from Newark riding out to Venus on a double hit of acid, cheerleaders from Scarsdale flapping their mescaline wings to the Temptations, pole vaulters from Queens snorting heaven up their noses, a great grinning bumping grinding crowd slick with sweat and hot thoughts about *whom* the evening might bring.

I called Beryl shortly before leaving work to say that I might stop at Stanley's for a quick beer and she said that would be just grand because she was going to cook yummy grape leaves stuffed with ground lamb for dinner. A lovely bottle of Chardonnay was chilling in the fridge, said Beryl, and later we could watch the telly, smoke a little hash, and make love in front of the eight-foot mirror we carried home from a junkshop on Second Avenue. I said that all sounded ever so ducky, that I couldn't wait to get home to our cozy little pad (which would be about 110 degrees when the sun went down), couldn't wait to sit 'round the table (if we'd had a proper table to sit 'round) and couldn't wait to chat about my day at the office (if the day hadn't been another endless hung-over haze in the morning, a dexadrine flight through the long afternoon).

But now I'm long past the point of caring about food, or even sex. Alfie, who walked out of Stanley's in a melodramatic huff, bringing his following to the Old Reliable, fills my shot glass and draws another beer chaser, palming the soggy dollar bill I've left on the bar, spinning toward the register, leaving a five in its place. I stare at Willy J., who is sitting at the far end of the bar, light reflecting off his greasy, conked hair, a black do-rag wrapped around his completely empty skull. Willy J. Pusher, a fixture of regal stupidity at the Old Reliable, fondling his pearl-handled switchblade, pushing the button that makes the steel spring loose with a nasty snapping sound. Willy never seems to tire of flicking his blade, never gets bored jabbing the tip of his knife into the wooden bar and plucking it like a string on his evil little harp.

I stare at Willy J., trying to burn holes through his feeble brain, to knock him off his barstool with my hateful thoughts. I glare at the back of his skull, thinking about Mary Catherine, alone on a smelly mattress in some cockroach-crawling pad, a six-month-old version of Willy floating inside her county Clare tummy. Once upon a time we laid in bed together, my face snuggled in her thick red hair, our bodies wrapped warmly beneath a quilt warm and friendly, she telling me stories about growing up in rural Ireland.

"Oh yes, me father was a great one for it," she would say. "With twelve wee children in the house and himself drinking up the food money. And then, come morning after he'd broken up the place drinkin' and fightin', raising his dirty old head from the floor to sing 'Top a the mornin', children. I never felt better in me life.' The bastard. The fugging old bastard. I should have taken the turf spade to his head for sure."

Looking at old, badly faded photographs and planning our trip. Ah yes, we'd be settled in by a turf fire after a day of walking by the Shannon, a bit of fishing, a picnic lunch of smoked salmon, cold spuds, a bottle of wine, more strolling to a quaint little thatched roof pub where the owner tells stories about rising up with the IRA in 1916, sings a song or two about killing the Black & Tans, and refuses our money because, he says, Mary Catherine's father, God bless his departed soul, was a grand old fellow the likes of which will not be seen in these parts again, then home, and reading Liam O'Flaherty's stories aloud, a tumbler of hot whiskey punch between us, a dog at our feet, the sea bubbling with schools of sliver fish, waves lapping to our very door, wee donkies braying to their lovers, sheep dancing on rooftops, wild horses serenading us with penny whistles.

"You hate Willy J. because he's black, that's all. Why don't you admit it?" Mary Catherine said one night shortly before Alfie shouted "Last Call."

"Fuck that, Mary," I said. "I've nearly been killed by gangs of black men three times. Stabbed in the face, beaten, close to being murdered when I was just fifteen years old. I woke up in the emergency ward and everybody was saying 'NIGGER NIGGER NIGGER.' The nurses, the doctors, my friends, the cops, my parents, everybody. 'NIGGER NIGGER NIGGER.' And I looked at my hands, swollen and bruised from blocking my attackers clubs, and I thought 'Wait a minute. They tried to kill me because I'm white.' I tried to talk them out of it, Mary. I said, 'Hey, you don't even know me. You don't even know who I am, man, where I come from. I'm not rich. My parents are poor, man. My whole fucking family is poor, man. My grandparents don't even have an indoor toilet. My kin lives down in the bottoms. Nobody has a goddamn thing in my family.'

"I was screaming, screaming for my life, Mary. Trying to tell them that I didn't hate *them*. Because I didn't. I really didn't. I had been taught to hate black people all my life, but for some reason I couldn't do it. My attackers said, 'WE WANT TO KILL SOME WHITE MOTHERFUCKER. WE WANT TO KILL SOMEBODY WHITE.' And they started stabbing me, Mary. And when I looked at my hands in the emergency ward I said 'Fuck this. Fuck all of this. We kill them because they're black. They wanted to kill me because I'm white. This is crazy, man. I don't believe in this. I don't accept this. I don't want to LIVE THIS SHIT anymore.' I had a revelation, Mary. Right there, laying in my own blood, spitting out bits and pieces of teeth, huge swollen spots all over my head, with a serious brain concussion and a lot of nightmares that still haven't gone away, Mary."

One night, I watched Willy and his friends dump a young woman in a doorway outside the Old Reliable. They'd shot her full of drugs in the backroom and pulled off her underwear, passing her from lap to lap. She was drooling and vomiting and they took her outside, tossed her into a doorway, and walked away. She was pregnant and all we could do was watch her stomach rise and fall, as though the fetus were trying to break out of its poisoned mother. We stood on the sidewalk watching the life draining out of her. The cops refused to drive her to Bellevue, the ambulence was coming from Georgia, and her breathing grew more feeble. We pleaded with and insulted the cops who ignored us and when it started to rain John covered her with his own coat. Then we walked away, because we didn't want to see her die. The pushers were already down the block, looking for someone else to con or kill.

"This used to be a great scene, Mary. Alfie, you, me, Beryl, John, Cris, Sarah, Allen. We just wanted to read our poetry, paint our pictures, get drunk, get laid, smoke a little dope now and then.

"And then along comes Willy J. and his chickenshit pusher friends, with their knives and guns and anyone who doesn't like them hates all black people on earth.

"Yeah, this was a great scene until Willy got here. Because you and I used to be lovers . . . used to be friends . . . we were going to Ireland some day . . . we were going to collect periwinkles when the tide went out, make love by a turf fire in the Ayan Islands, ride wild horses on the beach, row about in a currach. We were going to raise a pint or two in Brendan Behan's favorite pubs and put flowers on his grave, visit Yeats' tower in County Sligo, ride horses through the streets of Dublin, shouting out passages from *Ulysses* and *Finnegans Wake*, visit the birthplace of Synge, O'Failoin, O'Casey, snuggle up with a glass of hot whiskey, the North Sea roaring just outside our thatched cottage's door . . .

"Ah, fuck that stupid scumbag cocksucking waste case," I shouted. "I don't hate Willy J. because he's black," pounding my empty glass on the bar. "I hate him because he's a piece of scum, because he's donkeyshit, dogvomit, snakepiss, junkiescum, the scum of motherfucking earth."

Mary Catherine's hand landing flush on my cheek, burning through my romantic fantasies, through our friendship.

"Don't ever speak to me of it again. Never I tell you. Don't speak to me of *anything* ever again. I'll not be telling Willy what you think of him. And I'm advising you to leave it be yourself unless . . ."

"Unless what Mary Catherine? Unless I want to get killed?"

"I never said such a thing. I never would."

"You don't have to, Mary. I get the message."

Willy J. spins in and out of focus, in and out of the traps I lay for him, the slow sadistic ways I plan to kill him. Alfie sees me staring at Willy and tries to wave me off, shaking his head, pouring me another drink but I ignore him, getting up from my stool and moving toward the back room, brushing Willy J.'s arm and looking squarely into his Iguana eyes, his pointed little tongue flicking in and out, the switchblade lying open on his lap.

"Hey man," he hisses, "watch where you're goin'."

Man my ass you motherfucker you know my name so call it if you can remember your own mother's you know who I am you jiveass pimp smack-pushing piece of shit.

"Fuck you, Willy," I say, "and your mother too," turning my back on him and walking into the crunch on the floor, moving in with the crowd, alcohol pumping luxurious happiness through my veins, dancing with one of Alfie's transvestite friends and, I'm convinced, Alfie himself, pressing into women I've slept with and women I want to, the dancers in one gyrating knot, and when I slip through to the bar for a another drink a young black woman sitting with some of Willy J.'s friends winks and smiles at me and I walk over to her and say, "Yeah baby, I hope you're serious, cause where you want to do it?" And without a word she rises from her chair, yanking a knife from between her breasts and lifting it slow motion to strike at my chest and the jukebox wails "LOVE IS GOOD" I swing a chair at her head and something smashes against my skull "LOVE IS STRONG" and darkness carries me down I'm banged and kicked and slapped forward on a wave of fists chairs flying glasses and "WE GOTTA GET BACK WHERE WE STARTED FROM" glass shattering, Milly screeching in some distant place, Harold shouting for us to stop, and I'm kicked through a wave of curses landing on my hands and knees sliding face down onto the sidewalk, and John is bleeding from the nose and mouth and they are booting us in the ribs and smashing their feet into our faces, screaming **"Stab those motherfuckers stab them kill them stab the cocksuckers kill them now stab"** blood running from my own nose and mouth onto my hands and we are wounded bulls but the matadors don't move in for the kill, and my face is inches from John's I whisper, "They're gonna kill us man. We're gonna die," John's glasses stomped to tiny glitter shards and he takes a kick to the head "I'm gonna count to three John, then up, man, we're going to get up and run." ONE, TWO, THREE, the gauntlet breaking with our sudden head-down charge and we are flying above the pavement down third street toward Avenue C, and four blocks uptown, scrambling four flights of stairs to John's apartment, where I grab his lover's .22 pistol and head for the door, screaming that I'm going to kill Willy J. and his friends, John and others holding me down and later the phone ringing, ringing, tears rolling down John's blackened eyes when he tells us that Cris has been taken to Bellevue with two stab wounds in his chest, and only then do I remember who jumped in front of me and Willy J.'s assassin girlfriend. I remember that someone saved my life, and I feel very much like crying, but can't.

When I return to the apartment a week later Beryl is gone. My typewriter and the folder in which I keep my poems is lying at the bottom of the airshaft, the typewriter's keys sprung up, the roller tilted out of its cradle, a perfect still life for Salvador Dalí. Scattered across the floor of the airshaft, already half buried in garbage, stained with grease and ketchup, are forty or fifty of my poems—everything I've written in the past year. I will have to leave them there, unread by anyone except Beryl and myself, unpublished, unknown. The bathroom is looted and trashed, a solitary condom (Beryl and I never used them) floating in the toilet. The electricity is cut off, the phone is dead. Our eight-foot antique mirror, topped by wooden cherub's heads that smiled down upon our passion—Beryl on her knees shaking her great mane "Oh God look at you how big you look oh aren't we beautiful oh God look at us Oh let's come together"—the cherubs who had watched us watching ourselves, listened to us listening to ourselves, smashed to splinters, all in sad pieces, dead.

Not even a goodbye note this time.

Clairon, Iowa, '62.

Billy Hicks, the alcoholic who sat in the back seat of a sheriffs car with me, handcuffed and shaking with fear and rage as the car bobsledded down ice-covered highways, is wearing a pair of sequin-studded cardboard wings, his huge frame draped in a crisp white sheet, no shoes or socks on his great fat feet. He's supposed to be a Christmas angel. I follow him to the middle of the ward where a small Christmas tree twinkles, a crazy quilt of lights and decorations flung, it appears, angrily across its branches. Beneath the tree is a pyramid of shoeboxes, each marked with a red cross. A row of penguins, their heads newly shaved, shoes shined, clothes neatly pressed, sit on metal chairs facing the tree.

Across from the penguins a high school choir is preparing to sing, trying to hide their fear and disgust, glancing about the room, they think, surreptitiously. A young girl who surely plays the Virgin Mary in the Passion Play is staring at me, and when I return her gaze she blushes and averts her eyes, then steals another glance. I smile and, feeling cruel, wink at her. She blushes, quivers, stares into her palms. Someone giggles and the choir director raises his hands high over his balding head, pursing his lips, and tapping his foot three times.

Our visitors have lovely voices, well trained and wonderfully sincere. But the penguins, though massively drugged, have little patience. By the third song they are shuffling their feet and clapping their hands, one or two singing miles off-key. The choir sings louder, not realizing that the penguins think this is a contest. They too sing louder and even more off-key, one penguin stamping his feet, as though trying to put out a fire. Another is sobbing. The frantic choir director waves his singers higher. Frightened, their concentration broken, tone fragmented, and then a loud boom, followed by another, not cacophonous but basso profundo, Bach's organ, Casal's cello, confident and rising sure NOEL NOEL NOEL NOEL NOEL. Hicks towering above the room, his silver sequined cardboard wings drooping and his halo sliding to one side, his voice lifting through the roof, across the frozen fields, past farmhouses where boys and girls are playing tag in the snow and the barnyard animals lift their chapped noses to the wonderful aroma of apple pie and acorn squash and stuffed goose and . . . past suburbs, all the way to Fairlawns County Hospital, where Hicks and I lived until we were sent down to the snakepit.

Allison, head nurse at Fairlawns, hears the singing and weeps. The deputies who brought us handcuffed to the snakepit listen and feel strangely melancholy. Moved by Hicks' singing, Dr. Tadpole gathers up his family and, for the first time in years, attends mass at St. John's. Moleface, brushing his teeth with Colgate, joins in the singing. Ear Fetish, stuck in a massive depression for more than a month, prances across her living room in a short pink nightgown. Christmas and Jesus born in a manger. Jesus poor. Jesus performing miracles. Jesus walking on water. Jesus hanging on the cross. Jesus rising from the dead. Jesus with long cloven scars across his skull. Jesus with marble eyes. Jesus strapped to a chair, beaten with a rubber hose, shot full of insulin, electricity, Thorazine.

Hicks' voice rises higher and the choir stops singing; the orderlies emerge from their cubicles, laying their charts and syringes aside, commencing to sing. The penguins' eyes blink off and on with the lights, NOEL NOEL Hicks rising and now everyone joining in. The doctors in Timmy Tammy Too, their torsos buried in warm white sand, lay their whiskey sours aside and sing. On the back wards where the miserables are kept the straitjackets are removed, doors unlocked, manacles thrown aside, hands joined, singing. Even Dr. Hotchkins lays his shockbox aside, falls to his knees, and manages a reasonable facsimile of NOEL.

And then as quickly as it begins the singing ends and a great silence spreads through the ward. Hicks glances about in surprise, waking from a trance. Radiators hissing softly, snow pattering against the windows, the lights on our tree twinkling like tiny stars of Bethlehem.

"Thank you for allowing us to sing for you today," the director says, bowing and herding his choir toward the nearest exit. "We look forward to . . . seeing you . . . next . . ." but he disappears before completing his sentence.

"Now close your eyes and I'll give you a really big surprise," a stout nurse in a stiff-starched uniform squeals. Everyone closes their eyes. "Now hold out your hands. Now smile." The penguins grinning, grimacing, groaning. "Now here you are." She walks down

the line, placing one shoebox into each pair of outstretched hands. "*Now you may open,*" she says, the penguins opening their eyes. "*Now look inside.*" They look. Then slowly, methodically, they begin removing the contents—tubes of Colgate, cellophane-wrapped brownies, chocolate chip cookies, ballpoint pens, miniature bags of peanuts—and tossing them on the floor.

"*No, no, that's not nice,*" the nurse scolds. "*That's not what we're supposed to do with our presents.*" The penguins ignore her. Mesmerized or stoned on quaaludes, the orderlies laugh as the penguins stomp the contents of their shoeboxes into the newly polished floor. The penguins are giggling and skating on the mess and one goes down, then another, rolling and flailing back and forth across the ward. One penguin rips a string of lights from the tree and, wrapping them around his neck, races for the exit, tripping over an orderly's outstretched foot and giggling as he lies face down, bleeding profusely from the nose.

"*Let's get outa here before someone get's killed,*" Hicks shouts.

"*But Hicks, I'm not allowed . . .*"

"*Allowed my ass, junior. It's Christmas.. Besides, us alkies got the run a the place. Gave us keys to all the wards. Come and go as we please, kiddo.*"

CHAPTER 6

Afternoon Soirees

On Sunday afternoons we gather at John's apartment, shaking loose our hangovers with Bloody Marys and Benzadrine, reading the poems we've written that week, or works-in-progress. We discuss Baudelaire, Apollinaire, Verlaine, and we argue about whether poets can adapt the techniques of Cubist painters to their work. Albert, who carries a photo of himself and Albert Camus in his wallet, denounces the idiocy of American literature, the vulgarity of American art, the stupidity of all things American, with the possible exception of his friend John, who lived in Paris after serving in the army, speaks fluent French, has published two books of poems, cooks eight-course gourmet meals (which the Parisian gobbles without uttering a single *merde*), knows everything about jazz and classical music, and decorates his walls with erotic prints from, *mais oui oui,* a porno shop in Pigalle. Albert waves the photo of himself and Camus about, a talisman, perhaps, against our American stupidity.

We talk about Alfred Jarry, the drawf-sized playwright who lived *between* floors in Paris, carried loaded pistols in his belt, wrote *Ubu Roi,* an absurdist, experimental, play, and walked a lobster on a leash up and down the boulevards of the Left Bank. Alfie is reading, and rereading, *The Diary of Alice B. Toklas,* which he says is "very campy," and Albert announces that once upon a time he met Gertrude Stein in Paris, or that he knows someone who knew her in Rome, or that someone who knew her somewhere said something important to him once. Jimmy—we call him Squirrel Monkey because his arms and legs and neck are matted with a thick rust-colored bristle—declares that he saw Andy Warhol crawling down Bleecker Street last Friday night. Everyone yawns. Squirrel Monkey is a pathological liar and a real miser. He lives in a tiny walkup on East Fifth Street between Avenues B and C, and when I'm really down and out I crash there. He lets me sleep on his floor or his too-short couch, cooks me dinner— three golf balls he insists are potatoes, one goldfish which he manages to filet, three lettuce leaves, and four or five peanuts for dessert. With a "You have no idea how much this cost me" flourish, he opens a bottle of Bowery vintage wine, pouring a thimbleful for each of us, sighing with satisfaction. When I refuse his advances—so extravagantly paid for—Jimmy goes out cruising, returning with bruises and torn clothes. I never stay for breakfast.

John reads excerpts from Hugh Selby's *Last Exit to Brooklyn,* and then we argue about whether John Rechy, author of *City of Night,* is straight or gay, and whether it makes any difference, and if creativity and homosexuality are synonymous, and Jimmy turns to me and says:

"Well, anyway, when are you going to come out of the closet?"

"I'm out of the closet."

"No, I mean, don't you realize you would be a much better writer if you just . . ."

"Just?"

"You know what I mean."

"Have sex with men?"

"Allowed your true nature to flow."

"My true nature does flow."

"Maybe, but it would flow better if you stop repressing."

"What am I repressing?"

"Your true nature."

"My nature is true."

"You're gay, you just won't admit it."

"I can't admit what isn't true for me, Jimmy. I like gay men.

I even like you, Jimmy, but you don't turn me on. I don't want to have sex with men, that's all."

"Oh leave him alone," says Alfie, putting his arm around me. "He's mine anyway. We're getting married tomorrow. Going to have lots and lots of children. Live in a little stone house on the Delaware, with a great big fireplace, oak floors, and lots of antiques. You know, all that kind of silly shit to make us happy. So don't be making passes at him you little swish."

"No one's making passes, Alfie," Jimmy whines. "We're talking about human nature, that's what we're really talking about."

"About *his* nature."

"I was just trying to tell him that he doesn't really know what his nature is."

"I know what my nature is, but I can't help it, any more than you can, Jimmy."

"Who wants to help it," Alfie laughs. "I like my . . . as you put it . . . na . . . ture . . ."

"But isn't it true that most great writers and artists have been gay?"

"Oh God, not that again. How boring. Who knows, who cares?" Alfie sighs.

"It's important, because the straight world doesn't want people to know."

"The so-called straight world doesn't know what it wants *itself* to know. But who cares? Gay, straight, bi. If Warhol were a eunuch, or slept with elephants, what difference would it make? I'd still like his work, it would still be just too, too campy."

"So what you're trying to tell me, Jimmy, is that if I come out of the closet I'll be another Michelangelo, or maybe Shakespeare?"

"Maybe."

"But I won't, because there's only one Michelangelo. And one Shakespeare. They were geniuses, born that way, and there won't be any others like them, ever. And besides, whoever said they were gay."

"They were."

"How do you know?"

"I've read about it."

"Where?"

"I don't remember."

"Well, I might 'come out of the closet' if I thought it would make me a genius, but it won't, Jimmy. Whatever I've got I've got, but I don't know what the fuck it is yet."

"You don't have to get nasty."

"Sorry, Jimmy, I didn't mean to hurt your feelings. I'm just tired of this subject."

"Give him time," Alfie laughs, patting my back. "Some people are just slower than others. Besides, before he comes out of the closet he's got to know he's in. And you," waving at me, "still don't know that yet, do you Mr. Jones? Well, you'll find out on our honeymoon, that's for sure."

We talk about the Living Theater's productions (Siobhan had taken me to meet Judith Beck and her husband, Julian, hoping I could crash at their theater for a while, but fire inspectors were demanding that the anarchist camp-out between the theater aisles disband, else the city would close the building down altogether, so I found no shelter there). And there's always a few good stories about James Baldwin because he conquered the odds—racism, poverty, hatred of homosexuals—and now he writes good books and his books are selling and people are listening and it seems like everyone on the Lower East Side has gotten drunk or slept with, given or gotten help from Jimmy Baldwin.

We read our work and when we're drunk we talk about Camus' "There is but one truly serious philosophical problem, and that is suicide." Papa Hemingway, Sylvia Plath, Hart Crane, Virginia Woolf, James Dean, perhaps even Camus himself, the list is long and we ponder it often, intrigued by some strange and rather romantic notion that dying young is, somehow, heroic.

I read a poem I wrote after a rather gloomy walk down Second Avenue, called *Early Morning*.

> Steam
> fogging out, upward from
> gutters
> as a paper

flip flops in the morning
sadness
as feet clomping
in the stillness
an awning flapping
a mind slipping into fog and
flapping
It is all stillness, rushing
to the point of solitude
Noticing
that all has fled and come to
this
an overstuffed emptiness.

It isn't about suicide, and when I read it at the soiree everyone seems to like it very much and later that afternoon we walk to Stanley's where we drink until four in the morning and take a cab to Queens to the home of a young acid head existentialist whose parents are in Bermuda and we stay there for days, drinking all the booze, eating all the food, dancing to the new British group, the Beatles, leaving huge piles of dishes in the kitchen, the beds unmade, the bathroom caked in vomit and dried piss, and when our soiree finally ends we still have a great deal to talk about.

"God is dead," someone says at our next soiree and, "How do you know he's dead if you never saw him alive?" someone else says, and Jimmy says he's quite certain that God is gay. We read more poems, talk about art and suicide and sex, and Albert says that American politicians are all Fascists, and Jimmy reveals, because he's read it somewhere, that the Beatles are transvestites, and Alfie tells Jimmy that of course they are, and so are Lyndon Baines Johnson and Mick Jagger and Jim Morrison and Elvis Presley, and Jimmy complains that Alfie is just putting him on again. And even though we feel a shadow, cold and slippery, and one of Jimmy's Puerto Rican lovers gets drunk and drugged up one night and passes out on the floor of his wife's pad and she calls the FBI who cuffs his sleeping arms behind his back and sells him to the nearest Marine recruiter . . . even though we feel it lurking just beneath our merry surface, we pretend that Vietnam is just a small ache, a minor nuisance that will soon go away, and we keep on writing and painting and dancing and drug-taking and fucking.

We never talk about the war, even when Albert declares that Americans are barbarians, worse than Nazis, worse than, Oh mon Dieu, ever so much worse than the French when they were killing the Algerians or the Vietnamese, and we ignore him because he's just an arrogant Frog who thinks God looks like or may even be Robespierre, sitting on a giant artichoke-throne, stuffing himself with escargot and paté, guzzling wine and bestowing crowns of glory or quick trips to the eternal fire on men and women in little tri-color hats.

CHAPTER 7

Love

I was afraid Harold might not let me back in the Old Reliable, but he greets me warmly, shaking my hand, pouring out a large glass of whiskey "on the house" and trotting off to the kitchen for a plate of French fries. No, he says, Beryl hasn't been in for several days, not since the fight, he thinks. Beautiful girl, he says, but kinda nuts sometimes. Kinda. Something gets into her anyway. Yeah, Harold, something does. I lick the grease off the ends of my fingers, wash the fries down with whiskey. And Cris? He's o.k., I say. Told us a story when we went to see him in Bellevue. Said the orderlies were joking around. "Good thing that guy they brought in last night was already dead," said one orderly, "cause I couldn't find the oxygen nowhere, could you?" "Hell no. Nowhere," said the other. We laugh. Harold fetches more fries.

"Modigliani was tormented," Harold says, refilling my glass.

"Tormented, Harold?"

"Sure, all great artists are tormented."

"So all anyone needs to do to become a great artist is be tormented?"

"No, of course not. But think of it. If Modigliani or Vincent Van Gogh or Paul Gauguin walked in here right now, would we recognize them? No. Probably not. How do we know who's

who? Vincent might ask for a glass of wine, maybe something
to eat. Would he have money? Of course not. Would we think
he was just another bum? Of course. And what would happen? We'd be turning down one of the greatest artists of the
century. It's a crime what happens to artists. Hungry all their
lives, then someone comes along and buys their paintings for
a million bucks as soon as they die. It's not fair."

"If Modigliani walked in here, Willy J. would try to sell him
smack, turn him into a junkie, Harold."

"No, not Modigliani," Harold insists. "Van Gogh, maybe.
Paul Gauguin, no doubt. Never Modigliani."

A bookie paces up and down the bar, taking bets from the
afternoon crowd of Polish exiles. He writes nothing down,
collecting everything he needs to know—the horse's name,
the odds, the amount of money wagered—in his head. Within
minutes he's on his way to another bar, gathering more bets.
When he returns, he'll distribute the winnings and keep the
losses, all according to his memory which, if he wishes to
remain alive and healthy, must be photographic.

The bookie walks out and two policemen stroll in. Once
upon a time they were choirboys, with lovely blue eyes and
freckled little faces, but time has broken the veins in their
noses, turned their cheeks into jowls, chiseled deep grooves
into their foreheads. They remove their hats, place them on
the bar. Harold pours them each a double shot of whiskey,
no ice or water. They slug it down. Another triple shot. Slug
slug. Finally the biggest bull, a sergeant, holds his hand over
his glass and shakes his head.

"O.K., Michael, what it's gonna be?" Harold sighs.

"Be six bills this time, Harold," the bull answers, his voice
as flat as his eyes.

Harold opens his safe, puts six one hundred dollar bills in
an envelope and hands it to the sergeant, who holds it up to
the light, shaking it a couple of times, then stuffing it into
his tunic. The bulls nod, Harold nods. When they drive away,
Harold pours me another drink. "How about a sandwich?
It's on the house," he says. "That wasn't so bad. Believe me,
it coulda been worse, a lot worse. They coulda closed the
place down if they'd wanted to."

I stay in Beryl's apartment, broke and hungry (I'd gone

back to the office temp job after a week of drinking with Alfie and his friends but the supervisor, smelling my breath, told me to go home and sober up), writing poems by candlelight, hoping to hear the arrogant clack clacking of her high heels on the steps, dreading she might appear. Beryl and I furnished the place with orange crates and other junk we found in the streets. The windows don't have curtains, we sleep on a lumpy mattress on the floor, and the kitchen is being dismantled by cockroaches, but this is the first real home I've had in more than three years. I don't want to go back to the streets.

The landlord tapes eviction notices to the door, pounding and whimpering until I unhook the police lock, pull back the deadbolt, and snap several other latches, leaving the chainlock on.

"Beryl's gone," I say, peering through the two-inch opening.

"Gone?" the old lecher cries. "Gone to where?"

"Gone to a watery death," I chuckle.

"What do you say?"

"To the belly of a whale, to seaweed orgies with Moby Dick, to humping great white sharks, to bringing scores of blond-haired, blue-eyed, cockney-speaking sea cows into the world."

"What are you telling me?" he says, reaching his long avaricious fingers through the door and trying to pry it open. "What is that you are trying to tell me?"

"Just this," I shout, slamming the door on his hand.

Something strange is going on in our neighborhood. Every day there's less garbage in the gutters and fewer heaps of trash on the sidewalk. Every day, city workers push brooms up and down the curbs, while machines with great spinning wire wheels sweep round and round through the streets. The neighborhood is actually getting cleaner. The neighborhood is starting to shine. On Avenue D, workers unload truckloads of flowers, planting them in neat little patterns around the projects. They plant rows of trees and bushes, framing the concrete amphitheater the city just completed building in-between the projects.

At last the work is completed, and a string of limousines rolls to a stop on Avenue D. President Johnson's wife, "Lady

Bird," steps out of one, wearing a sundress and wide-brimmed hat. A swirl of people escort her to a podium in the amphitheater. Puppy and I are sitting in the third row, waiting for the First Lady to begin her remarks. I smell pot, but can't believe anyone would light up in front of so many FBI agents, Secret Service agents, detectives, military intelligence agents, New York City cops, highway patrolmen, but there he is in the back row, puffing away on a long-stemmed pipe, his snake curled around his neck, a real guitar across his lap, grinning and waving to imaginary friends. Perhaps he really can become invisible, because no one seems to notice Zarro, even when he starts singing "The Star Spangled Banner" in the middle of Lady Bird's talk.

"Oh my," says the First Lady, "I just like to think of y'all out here on a nice starry evening, enjoying a cool summer breeze and watching a play by Shakespeare or Euripides." Someone giggles. People roll their eyes and shrug. Zarro sings "Home On The Range." Puppy yawns. The President's wife smiles, and continues to read from a stack of note cards. A teenage Puerto Rican I know from the neighborhood turns to me. "What's she tripping on, man?" he asks. "I wish I had some a that shit, man."

City workers return the next day, but with shovels this time instead of brooms. They dig up the trees and throw them on their truck. Then they dig up the flowers. They leave the amphitheater, but don't put up any notices about a premiere performance of "King Lear" or "Oedipus Rex." They don't pick up the garbage for another two weeks.

"Beryl's in Manhattan State," Alfie says, "taking part in this new program. You just go up there, tell them you're an alcoholic, and voila, they give you LSD. Some shrink thinks he can cure alcoholics by turning them into acid heads. Clever idea, very campy. Strange, isn't it? You drop acid out on the street and they bust you for it. But in the psych hospital, it's o.k. She says it's fun. She gets high every day. Stoned out of her mind. And just for letting them watch her flip out, they give her a room, books, food, and maybe even money. One of the doctors asked her to be his mistress, but she claims she told him that would be unethical."

"Unethical," I laugh. "Beryl?"

Alfie lights up a joint, inhales and hands it to me.

"Hear about those kids last week?" he asks.

"Yeah, Alfie. Someone threw them off the roof."

"I don't know who did it. Heard it was junkies," Alfie sighs.

"So much killing, Alfie."

"So much life too. Ironic," says Alfie.

"Life and death."

"And love," I cough.

"Strong stuff isn't it?"

"Yeah, Alfie. Too strong for me."

"Love," Alfie giggles. "My my, aren't we feeling deep today? Or just a little horny?"

"Fucking kids, Alfie. Why would anybody kill kids?"

"Who knows? Why do people do anything? Get up. Eat. Have sex. Go to work. Sometimes I wonder, really, about all of it. It's so . . . mundane . . . so Pavlovian . . . Who knows, maybe we're just dogs in human bodies. So simple to train. You know, two barks for a bone. Three barks to go outside. Bark bark. We think we're talking, but all we're doing is barking. Maybe," he adds, giggling, "that's why people like 'doggie style' so much."

Alfie wears blue jeans and a newly starched white shirt. On his left wrist, a Native American bracelet made of turquoise stones embedded in silver. Around his neck, a silver heart-shaped locket engraved with his initials, and a photograph of his Puerto Rican lover inside. I've held Alfie in my arms when he was mourning the death of one of his lovers— the first time I had ever touched another man except to punch, shove, wrestle, tackle, or beat him. I've spent the night at his apartment, sleeping between him and his lover, yet he has never tried to touch me; not even when, drunk, depressed, and desperately lonely, I might have wanted him to.

Alfie is an incorrigible dilettante, always working on a new novel, though he knows nothing about writing, always painting a new canvas, though he knows even less about art. He starts dancing lessons, switches to singing, and enrolls in acting lessons all within one week. He tries out for parts in plays, never getting them, but undaunted still plans his debuts in Hollywood and on Broadway. He drags home a half ton of clay, but soon gives up being a sculptor, and begins flute lessons.

I love Alfie because he is a dreamer who can transform the most depressing day into pure possibility. He can turn his apartment into a stage, an enchanted forest, an Academy Awards ceremony, a dressing room, anything he wishes it to be. And it is exciting to be there with him, to become child-like, if not a child, again. When I'm with Alfie, there is no yesterday or tomorrow, just the moment, pure and fantastic and never meant to last. Just the now, grand and exciting as he, or we, choose to make it.

Julie Trees balances on the edge of harikari, Siobhan hides inside catatonic cocoons, Beryl cons her way to Nirvana, and I chase shadows in and out of drunken cul-de-sacs. Yet Alfie, who was forced to pack up his bags and stand beside the highway, thumb pointing toward the void, lives with Dionysian intensity, as though each day might be his last, and each hour is a new beginning. I love Alife because, just before I fell into the clutches of Dr. Frybrain, I too experienced being fully alive. I can remember, though I can no longer feel, crossing that great animistic plain where everything—the birds, fish, trees, even the rocks—spoke to me. Before lockups and pills and shock treatments, I can remember being an acorn, germinating, growing into a tree. I once stored sunshine in the marrow of my bones. I didn't need sleep or food. The rain nourished me. I rose and fell with some inner tide, not just exploring but *living* life's mystery.

I love Alfie for showing me what I might still recover—that there is life after death, even here on planet Earth. To Alfie, each day is a reprieve from disappointments, hardships, losses. Each day is a veritable resurrection. I've seen him standing by his window at dawn, playing like a kitten with the sun's golden braids, as though he had never seen such a wonder before, as though—he would say—the world were being created at that very moment.

One afternoon in Central Park we found a tiny bird alongside the trail. It was hopping about in all directions and desperately chirping, but no one stopped to help it. Alfie knelt before the wounded creature, wrapping it in his hanky, its beady little head protruding, and we raced for home, hailing a cab on Fifth Avenue, bounding up the stairs to his apartment, placing the bird in a box, giving it milk, bread, a beetle shell retrieved from the fire escape. When it died three days later, Alfie wrapped his friend in a piece of yellow silk, read passages from Loren Eisley's *The Immense Journey,* and wept as the plastic coffin floated down the East River.

I take the subway to 125th Street, walk crosstown a few blocks, and wait for the bus to Manhattan State Hospital. The bus is crowded with poor Black and Puerto Rican women, balancing plastic bags and children and purses on their laps, staring dolefully out the windows. Halfway over the bridge the bubbling in my lower intestine starts, working its way up to my chest and into my throat. I want to scream for the driver to stop, to leap from the bus window and swim back to Harlem. Something will give me away, I'm sure of it. Some mannerism, some inflection, some way that former mental patients have of speaking. Sweat rolls over my ears and down my neck. My hands shake and Beryl, dressed for afternoon tea and waving a pink Japanese parasol, is waiting at the bus stop.

"Silly boy," she scoffs. "You don't have to be afraid here. This isn't Clarion. No one's going to hurt you. They don't know," she teases, "that you're an ex-mental patient. You look like a perfectly ordinary psychotic to me. Besides, they actually give you psychedelic drugs here, for free. It's ever so much fun."

We walk hand-in-hand through the grounds of the hospital, standing now and then to look downriver, or to embrace. We spread a little picnic on the grass, some cheese and crackers she had pilfered, a bottle of wine I had "borrowed" from a friend's apartment, a couple of apples. I close my eyes and run my hand over Beryl's newly shaved legs, hesitating when I feel the warm dampness through her cotton panties. My hand moves across her marble stomach, playing momentarily with her navel, pinching her nipples, both hands sliding Beryl's underwear over her knees and around her ankles, tossing her bra and panties aside and she yanking at my own trousers and we are naked still wearing our shoes and I am inside of her so stunningly fast, locking our mouths, already rushing into surge, Beryl biting my ear so hard that I scream "I can't help it Beryl I'm coming Beryl I'm coming I can't stop" and she is thrusting her tongue in and out of my ear hard whispering, "OH GOD, you bastard you dirty little bastard OH GOD I LOVE OH GOD I LOVE YOU YOU OH GOD," sobbing now, her legs clinging to my middle and already my poor indecent wilting, "OH don't leave me yet not yet stay inside of me OH it feels so good," and somewhere, far off in the dreamworld first, then louder, clapping and cheering and when we roll sideways still locked together we can see them standing in the windows of the alcoholic ward, windows and windows, jammed with male patients, laughing clapping, giving us a standing ovation.

We pull on our clothes and look for a more secluded spot. A squad car is parked under a tree, two cops sleeping in the front seat.

"Our great protectors," Beryl laughs.

I run my fingers through her long blond hair, across her perfect lips, her straight white teeth, her aquiline nose, her dangerously blue eyes. And suddenly I'm overwhelmed with jealousy and sorrow, unable to bear the idea that another man will touch her, has ever touched Beryl the way I have. I want her to love me. I want her to belong to me. I want to possess her beauty. I want to love her.

"Leave with me now, Beryl," I say. "Who's going to stop you? You're not committed. You checked yourself in voluntarily, didn't you?"

"Where would we live?"

"I don't know, we'll find someplace."

"Nonsense, love. I don't want to live in a cardboard box, I don't want to sleep on rooftops, I won't eat in Bowery missions, and I refuse to sell my precious blood in those sleazy 'banks' you frequent. Jesus, five dollars for a pint of *my* corpuscles. You could get a lot more than that for your cute little ass, luv. Not likely, I tell you. I'm worth more, a bloody lot more than that. Maybe you can do that for the rest of your life, but not me."

"I'll get a job."

"You hate doing menial work."

"I'll find something I like."

"What, love? It drives you mad. I'm willing to support you while you write, but you hate me for doing it."

"We haven't tried."

"And we won't."

"Why not?"

"Because you just don't care, that's why."

"About what, Beryl?"

"About things like a quaint little cottage in Cornwall, with three cheeky kids, a sheepdog lying by the fire, head plopped in the kiddies' laps and all of us snuggled up together watching the telly. Oh, wouldn't it be lovely, lov . . . i . . . ly. I love you, but I know you're incapable of loving me, or anyone else for that matter. Besides, you're so bloody busy feeling sorry for yourself that you can't . . ."

"Can't?"

"You can't *feel* what anyone else feels, because you're right up to your neck in self-pity, love, and you don't even know it. You can't see that other people suffer too, just like you do, a lot of them a great deal more. Good God, do you really think you're the only human being who ever fell out with their family? Look at Toby. When he writes home, the letters are returned unopened. His parents might as well stamp QUEER on the back of the envelope. Even his own brother disowned him. Mind you, we've all got our crosses to carry. We're all paying some price for the way we're living. I haven't seen my own family for ten years. Probably never will again. But so what? What's so great about the family? Blood's thicker than water, my ass. You think you're the only one whose family did you harm? All families harm their children, even the good ones. That's the real purpose of the family, to break their children's spirit so they'll become well-adjusted fools and idiots like their own dear old parents. You hate yourself, ducky, so how on earth could you ever love me?"

Beryl kept at it, hurling invective across the blanket on which we sat, and for once I sat quietly, trying to understand what she was saying, wishing I knew why we couldn't just find work, an apartment, marry, have children together. Beryl was the most beautiful woman I had ever met, a virtuoso in bed, a veritable textbook of kinky innovations, weeping with pleasure when I came in her mouth, coming loud and hard the instant I entered her from behind, moaning with narcissistic joy watching her own body twist and bend and writhe in the mirror. When she told stories, Alfie and his groupies would sit at her feet, excited, enchanted, attentive. She could create a Cinderella gown out of a bundle of rags, turn yesterday's scraps into a six-course meal, recall verbatim anything she read, write Chekhovian short stories, yet Beryl was chasing her own shadows, driven by some strange inexplicable urge to tread the edge of the void on thin existential wires, indifferent to, even contemptuous of, the consequences of falling.

Since her exile from Britain, Beryl has relied on cunning and guile, chutzpah and blarney, selling her charm, wit, and good looks for a night of drinking, a good meal, a few days or a few weeks off the streets. Squeezed into her bright red dress, a little blue bow tied in her hair, Beryl can hustle even the toughest New York bartender, winking and smiling, imitating cockney accents, leaning into her drinks so the poor man will have a spectacular view of her cleavage, wagging her extraordinary body over to the jukebox and swaying her ass while pumping nickels into the slot.

When Beryl resurfaces after disappearing into the mean streets, she always tells the most wonderful stories:

She met a man on the subway who was dying of cancer and who pleaded with her to accompany him to the hospital. She did, and there she remained for one week, holding the poor bloke's hand and weeping, though she did not know exactly why, while he slowly expired. "Look," she would say, pulling a wad of money from her purse. "This was all the poor fellow had, and the nurses gave it to me. Ever so kind, don't you think?"

On yet another occasion Beryl claimed that her supervisor suggested they dine together at the woman's uptown penthouse. They enjoyed a lovely dinner (in Beryl's stories there are always grand dinners, most often *cuisine Francaise*)—several rounds of cocktails, then raw oysters, leg of lamb, a salad Niçoise, chocolate mousse, two full bottles of a century-old white wine, snifters of 1846 cognac after dinner—but when Beryl tried to leave for her own humble home at 2:00 a.m.

the woman commenced locking all the doors and threatened to commit suicide.

"Oh it was very tense," said Beryl, rolling her eyes and wringing her hands for emphasis. "I tell you. There I was, all alone with this insane woman. Listening to her scream. Wondering why the bloody peelers didn't knock in the door. Three days and nights.

"'Kill me,' she said. 'Please Beryl. I want you to do me a favor. Just take this knife and kill me.'"

"'Tomisina,' I said. Oh God, yes, that really was her real name. Tomisina O'Brien. Another Celtic lunatic. You would have adored her.

"'You've got so much to live for, Tomisina.'

"'About as much as a leper in Calcutta.'

"'You're so pretty, love.'

"She was a veritable troll."

"'You're so kind, my pet.'

"She was a bloody overseer, straight out of Dickens.

"'Everyone at work loves you, my little lamb.'

"We all despised her.

"'You've got a great future ahead of you Tomisina.'

"She would probably wind up a bloody bag lady like Siobhan.

"Finally she fell asleep and I made my escape, taking her coat, an ankle-length mink, because she had thrown mine off her balcony in a fit of pique."

After each one of these ridiculous accounts, I would commend Beryl on her story-telling ability.

"You really should write novels, Beryl. You've got such an incredible imagination, and you lie with such conviction. Either write for a living or go into acting. I really have to admire the way you put your heart into these stories. Sometimes I'm almost convinced they really happened."

"I'm not lying," she would insist. "That's exactly what happened. I was terrified. Fifty stories up in the air with a madwoman. My hands are still shaking. I can't sleep. I must have lost ten pounds. I ought to have Tomisina arrested for kidnapping. And listen to this. When I next saw her at work, she acted as though nothing happened. Nothing. 'Good morning, Beryl,' she says. 'I hope you had a lovely weekend.'"

"Great short story, Beryl. Well crafted. Held my interest. Fine ending."

"You obviously don't believe me, do you? Where do you think I was, out screwing some stockbroker just to make a few bucks?"

"Probably."

"You dirty little bastard."

"Just tell the truth."

"I am."

"You don't know how to tell the truth, Beryl."

"Look who's talking, the world's greatest bullshit artist. Have you seen *Billy Liar*? You really must, you know, because the movie's based on *your* life. The main character is *you*. He fits you to a tee."

Clouds scuttle overhead, dipping their fluffy tails, it seems, toward Beryl and me. I hand her the near-empty bottle of wine, watching her drain it and wishing I had never come here.

"Beryl," I say, "I'm leaving town for a while. Todd says I can work highrise construction if I come down to D.C. Make good money, maybe save a little, come back to the city, get an apartment."

"You're going to leave me here?"

"I'm not leaving you. I just have to get off the streets, Beryl. You remember that little hippie chick from Ohio, the one I warned to keep her windows locked? She said her pad was too hot at night, laughed at me, called me paranoid. Last week I saw her in the park, both of eyes black and blue, her nose broken, lips all swollen. She woke up with some guy right on top of her, and when she screamed he nearly killed her. All these kids walking around the neighborhood barefoot, trying to act like they know the fucking streets, copping drugs from piranha like Willy J."

We talked about the time Beryl pawned an eight hundred-dollar ring, a pearl circled by diamonds, for thirty dollars and we went to the bodega and bought three chickens and four six-packs of Guinness Stout and invited our friends over for a party and she cried for a week because the ring belonged to her grandmother and the pawnbroker was a sniffling little swine, and we lamented the signed copy of W.B. Yeats we exchanged for a bottle of gin and a frozen turkey so that we could have a proper Thanksgiving but . . .

"You smashed my typewriter, Beryl. Threw my poems down the airshaft, and left a rubber floating in the toilet just to let me know what you'd been doing."

"I waited for you to come home, but you couldn't leave your faggot friends."

"Don't talk about Alfie that way. You know you love him, and he loves you."

"He's a little fairy, that's what he is."

"What's that make you?"

"A woman."

"A whore, if you want to start calling people names."

"Oh for God's sake. At least try to be original. I just felt . . . well . . . a little crazy when you didn't come home."

"Like I felt when you disappeared. How many times, Beryl? Do you remember?"

"Once, maybe twice."

"I've lost count, Beryl. So have you."

"I thought you loved the city."

"I do love it, Beryl, but I'm back on the streets again. So are you. The landlord finally brought the cops in and kicked me out. I quit the temp agency, and I'm broke, and have run out of places to stay. Siobhan's taken in half the junkies in New York, and . . ."

"Why don't you just go home?"

"What home?"

"Back to Iowa. Take your chances. Forgive your family. Start over."

"Why don't you, Beryl?"

"You know perfectly well why I don't. My family exiled me. They banished me from England. But yours, well, they want you to come home, ducky. You're always showing me those letters in which your dear mummy pleads for her prodigal son's return."

"Yes, so they can lock me up again. She still insists I need 'help,' which means another trip to the loonybin, maybe more shock treatments. I'll die first. I said I would never see my family again, and I meant it. They tried to kill me. They still want to kill me. I'm not ready to die in some goddamn snakepit."

"I'm sorry. I just thought, well, how long can you stay angry at them?"

"As long as the sun rises and sets, Beryl."

"But it's killing you, not them."

"I'm more alive than I would be in Fairlawns or Clarion."

"Depends on how you define life, now doesn't it, love?"

"I'm not locked up, that's what life is."

"Ah, love, but there's other ways to be locked up. Anyway, how's Cris? Alfie said you started a row in the pub and Willy J.'s girlfriend tried to cut your heart out."

"He's o.k. She stabbed him in the chest a couple of times but the wounds weren't that deep."

"They catch her?"

"Catch her, Beryl? She was sitting at the bar the very next day, laughing about it. Said, 'I hope the white mother-fucker dies.'"

"Jesus. In London the peelers would have her in jail by now."

"This is New York City, love. Things don't happen that way here. Cops get paid off and everything's cool."

"Alfie said you were going to shoot Willy J."

"I would have."

"How romantic. Then you'd be in prison, and I'd have to visit you. I'd bring little picnic lunches and we could make love in your cell, wouldn't that be fun. We might have to allow the guards to watch, but *tant pis, J'mien fous, c'est la guerre.* Will you write to me?"

"Of course."

"You will not."

"I promise."

"Promise," Beryl laughs. "Your promises are about as good as . . . Lyndon Johnson's."

"About as good as yours, Beryl," I say, pressing her close and stroking her back.

"Come now, love. You got all you're going to get today," she laughs.

"I'll write to you, Beryl."

"Bugger off, will you," she says, laughing and wagging away. "I'll never hear from you again."

I watch her go, feeling empty and alone, wishing we could make love again, yet excited to be leaving her behind. I care about Beryl and sometimes, in the heat of our lovemaking, I even want to say the words she begs to hear. I want to shout "I LOVE YOU," or just "THANK YOU." Beryl accepts the human body, her own and others, as something profoundly sensuous and beautiful. She scoffs at my Bible Belt agonizing, insisting that God is a voyeur, that He likes watching human beings weep with pleasure, enjoys hearing mad passionate lovemaking, wants everyone to experience cataclysmic orgasms.

"After all," Beryl says, "when he was playing around with clay, or whatever it was he used to make the first man and woman, he didn't have to give us sex organs, now did he? What good is that thing you've got dangling on you, except for pleasure? What on earth does anyone need with a vagina, except to give happiness to one's lover, and to oneself? If God just wanted us to have babies, he could have made us so we could deliver them out of our mouths, or our ears, perhaps some opening in our stomachs. But he gave me a clitoris, not a hole in my stomach, and what on earth does a clitoris have to do with bringing children into the world? Nothing whatsoever, that's what. If God didn't want our lovers to play with us, if he didn't want women to come, he wouldn't have given us that precious little button, would he now, love?

"Sin," she laughs. "What is sin? Just the yak yaking of some old codger who can't get it up anymore, that's all. God's up there all right. But He's not wasting his time seeing who's being naughty and good. He's not keeping a list and checking it twice. Not at all, love. He's up there on a great white fluffy cloud, making love to all those beautiful angels. That's what you hear when it thunders. And that's what you see when there's lightning. Love sparks flying from cloud to cloud. The heavens just heaving with one great collective orgasm. Just imagine what great fun they must be having right now, while you're feeling guilty for enjoying sex.

"You see," she taunts, "you're just afraid that once you're

inside me I won't give it, I won't give *you* back. You think that while we're making love, I'll take your precious little thing away from you. That I'll devour you with my cunt. That I won't give you back to yourself. Don't worry, luv. I've never met a man who doesn't have that very same problem. That's why you men are all so childish, so desperately insecure. That's why you want to possess us, to own women, even though you don't ever really love us."

The Greyhound backs out of its stall in Port Authority and plunges into the Lincoln Tunnel, surfacing into the New Jersey sunshine. I press my nose to the glass, but the city is a mirage, fading quickly away. One night, watching Julie Trees melt crystals of amphetamine in a teaspoon, I asked her if she had ever been in love. "Love?" she scoffed. "That one's simple, Cowboy. Love is a four-letter word. Like fuck, or suck, or duck, or luck, or muck, or buck. Just four plain old letters strung together. The rest is in your imagination, Cowboy. A deadly little seed planted in our skulls and pretty soon it starts to grow, cutting off our circulation, shutting down the oxygen, until what we've got up there is just the same old collection of bullshit everyone else does. Until that once-great sponge, that superbrain that could store the universe if we just had the guts to use it, which you obviously don't, Cowboy, turns into a dried up gourd. See, that's what most people've got on their shoulders, Cowboy, just gourds full of cliches and platitudes that rattle when they walk. You can hear them. Just stand on any corner watching people go to work some morning. You'll hear gourds. Millions of them, Cowboy. All rattling to the same nursery rhyme. 'I . . . LOVE . . . YOU'. That's the most dangerous expression in the world, you dig Cowboy? I'd rather have someone point a gun in my face. I'd rather hear 'I'll . . . kill . . . YOU' than those three deadly little words."

Julie poured the liquid amphetamine into her syringe, tied off, and jammed the needle into a vein on the inside of her thigh. Before the rush hit, I walked out, leaving the door open. I walked down Avenue C to a rooming house on East 4th Street, climbed six flights of stairs and lay on the cot I was renting, in the kitchen, for six dollars a week. I lay awake most of the night, listening to cockroaches play tag up and down the walls, and the beating of my own confused heart. Each time my family locked me up in a psychiatric ward, they said it was because they loved me. Each time Dr. H. gave me another elecro-shock treatment, he was expressing my family's love. When the family clergyman visited me on the eve of my being sent to the snakepit, he said, "Let's pray to the God of love." When I refused he urged me to always remember how much God and my family loved me.

The cot was narrow, hard, uncomfortable. There were no windows in the tiny kitchen, no air. I was lying in a coffin. Awake in my own grave. God asked Abraham to show his love by sacrificing his son, Isaac. God loved the world so much that he sacrificed his own begotten son, Jesus. Jesus died because he loved his disciples. His heavenly father watched his son die slowly, painfully, Christ's hands and feet nailed to a wooden cross so that human beings would understand the meaning of love. If you love others, sacrifice them. If you love yourself, sacrifice yourself. If you love God, drink his son's blood, eat his son's flesh. Love is drinking someone. Love is eating someone. Love is dying so that those you love can live after you, drinking your blood, eating your flesh. Love is putting your son or daughter on the alter and sliding a knife across their throat. Love is cannibalism. Love is dying. Love is killing.

I laid on my cot, recalling how Johnny's parents came to Clarion to take him home for a weekend leave. He seemed to be doing fairly well when he left the hospital, but after a few days he returned in a basket, sniffling and muttering, his bones turned to water, his brain sucked dry. Johnny's parents patted his thirty-five-year old head, handed his belongings to the orderly and said, with remarkable cheerfulness, "Take care of him. He's our son. We love him so."

The bus pulls into Baltimore, groans on toward Washington, D.C. "Real love," says Beryl, "is being able to feel someone else's pain, something you just can't do." Perhaps, Beryl, but I'm not going to sharpen my sacrificial knife. I do not wish to eat your flesh. I'm not willing to construct an altar. I refuse to drink your blood. You are not Abraham, I'm not

Isaac. I am not Jesus. You are not the Virgin Mary. "I love you," Beryl screams, crushing my ribs with her Olympian legs, drowning me in her tears. My heart constricts. We lie together, motionless, spent, galaxies apart. "I love you," she whispers. "I love you too Beryl," I reply, unable to form the words. Beryl shuts her eyes. "Maybe we should build a cross," I say. "I'll buy some nails, teach you how to use a hammer." Beryl stops crying. She strokes my face, kisses my forehead, whispers in my ear. "Poor baby," she croons. "Close your eyes now, poor thing. Come now, luv, I won't say that again. I didn't mean to frighten you. I promise."

CHAPTER 8

Men

T*he boy was two inches taller than me and a grade ahead so I swung at the bridge of his nose and he held his hands under the bleeding but couldn't stop it and he started to cry and I hit him in the face warning him never to look at or speak to me on or off the playground and I laughed at him and turned my back and strutted off with my pals. It felt really good to be an eight-year old man.*

"Junior," the foreman laughs when I stumble onto the 14th floor, drenched in sweat, knees shaking like a newborn calf's, "you look like you been eatin' too much pussy over the weekend. Best stop that, hon. It'll kill your brain cells. Make you dumber'n hell. Read about it in a magazine. I ain't lyin', sugar. That's a true fact."

Johnny Lee pushes his red stetson back on his head and do-si-do's to the edge of the deck, standing on a plywood gutter that rings the floor we're working on. He closes his eyes, the tips of his boots hanging out over the edge, the plywood wobbling. Johnny rocks back and forth on his heels, leaning into space, defying gravity. Nails loosen, boards crackle and pop, chunks of the gutter spiral away and the foreman dances backward, laughing and waving his cigar at fate.

"Man's nuts," say the carpenters. "Got that scar on his face

113

in a Virginia roadhouse. Usta to hang out in them places. Usta fight a lot. Get his ass kicked, get throwd in jail every damn weekend. Good man, Johnny Lee Barnes. Daddy was a miner all right. West Virginia real fine boy. Best damn foreman ever was, but don't go fuckin' with him. Man ain't dumb. Treat Johnny right, he'll do the same back. Cross his ass, and you'll be one sorry sonofabitch. Get to drinkin' on the weekend, law throws your ass in jail, long's you're a good worker Johnny don't care where you been. Just pick up your toolbox and go get back to work. Fightin' with your woman, don't mean nothin'. Done bailed him out a jail a time or two myself."

Johnny takes a sandwich and a rumpled newspaper out of his lunchbox. "Well," he says, "I'll bet you don't know why Hitler killed all them Jews? I never did neither 'fore last night. You see, old Adolf was a queer. That's right. Queer as a three-dollar bill. It's all here," tapping the paper. "That's why he done it. I ain't lyin'. Hitler liked to suck men's cocks, but he didn't want nobody to know, so that's why he went and killed so many people. Just couldn't admit that he was a fairy 'stead of a man."

When the crane breaks down, Johnny Lee leans over the edge of the deck, screaming "COME ON, LET'S GET IT GET IT GET IT LETS GET IT BOYS GET IT." Laborers and carpenter's helpers form a human chain from floo to floor, passing along sheets of plywood, boxes of nine-penny nails, hundreds of 3 x 4's and 4 x 6's until our arms ache, our legs buckle, tears stream down our faces and we curse and moan but can't stop and Johnny keeps screaming until the whistle blows at 4:00 p.m. and when Johnny asks for volunteers to work overtime no one even says yes, or no. We just walk away.

By the end of the day my eyeballs are sunburned, the bones in my feet have collapsed, my kneecaps are broken. I want desperately to sit down on the bus back to Washington, but all the seats are taken. My hands are covered with cuts and bruises, my shins are scraped and scabby. Hammers and skill-saws echo inside my skull. My skin is fried to a brittle crisp. I smell like sawdust, blood, sour milk, and fear.

"'Fraid a heights, junior?" Johnny asks, the day after I nearly fall to my death.

"Hell no, Johnny."

"You mind working out on the edge, sugar?" the day after I nearly get blown over the side.

"Hell no, Johnny."

"Like workin' high-rise, hon?" the day after the craneman drops a pile of steel rods on one corner of the deck and the men panic, dropping their tools and running for safety.

"Hell yes, Johnny."

The bus is gridlocked. I bend over a young office worker, staring at the newspaper on her lap.

President Johnson tells Congress we are going to win this war.

Vietcong attack near Saigon repulsed with minor American losses.

North Vietnamese overrun Special Forces camp, casualties light.

I lean way over, lips almost touching the woman's shoulder, eyes locking onto her breasts, dripping sweat across the President's face. Drip, a bull's-eye on LBJ's forehead. Drip, a bull's-eye on his nose, left eye, cheek, forehead. The bus jerks forward, stops. The office worker ignores me, closing her newspaper and staring into the traffic. An elderly black woman rings the bell and the driver stomps on the gas, passing S.E. Third Street where we want to get off, squealing to the curb three blocks away. He does this every night.

Beryl is lying on the bed when I return from work, reading Lawrence Durrell's *Justine.* For several weeks we ran a merry little scam—my calling collect from a phone booth in Washington, D.C., to a phone booth on the grounds of Manhattan State Psychiatric Hospital. We talked for hours, and when the operator called back to tell us the charges (sometimes Beryl called to my phone booth), we just dropped the phone and walked away.

We whispered into the receiver, promising to be more loving, more understanding, more honest. Sending great expectations across the wires, Beryl swearing that she would stop drinking, get a steady job, practice monogamy when she got

115

to Washington. My assuring her that I would do all of that and more.

We would save our money and return to New York, find a cozy brownstone overlooking Tompkins Square Park, fill the windows with geraniums, sew lace curtains, furnish a real living room with Persian rugs and antique tables spread with copies of *The New Yorker* and *Atlantic*. We'd have a Steinway piano and giant Egyptian vases and original Picassos and Alfie and John and all our friends would visit for cocktails and proper teas. I would write poetry. She would write short stories. We would clip recipes from *The New York Times,* cook game birds in white wine, buy a miniature white dog, go window shopping in the Village and ice skating in Rockefeller Plaza. We would attend Broadway plays and concerts at Carnegie Hall, picnic on Camembert and wine at the Cloisters, weekend on Fire Island, summer at the Cape. We would take up a hobby (perhaps stamp or coin collecting), adopt a Bolivian orphan, do volunteer work at thrift shops and soup kitchens, go to confession, say our prayers, be faithful. We would stop chasing shadows.

Beryl lays her book aside, stretching her legs and fluffing up the pillow. "I stink," I say, starting to undress. "No, you smell like a man," she whispers, leading me down the hall and into the shower, where we lather one another under the hot spray and she guides me gently inside her with one hand, still washing my hair with the other, and the suds roll over and between us and later we lie together in our furnished room, on clean sheets, safe and warm and timeless, then out for a walk in the neighborhood, ordering dinner in a Chinese restaurant where one of the waiters has fallen in love with Beryl. When he sees her he nearly collapses with joy, leading us to her favorite table by the window. She is wearing a black mini-skirt, a pair of Peter Pan booties, a plain white T-shirt, no bra. Tonight her eyes are a deep, wet, mossy green. Her blond hair curls over her shoulders, and when she opens the menu her breasts rise, the nipples hard and teasing through her tight cotton shirt. She sits with her legs wide apart, giving the poor waiter a glimpse of heaven.

The waiter stumbles on the carpet, dropping our eggrolls. He forgets to bring my Moo Shu Pork, forgets to bring our tea. Beryl tells bawdy stories about Britain's royal family and he barks with pleasure. She lifts a clump of lo mein noodles from her plate, slowly sucking them from her chopsticks, and the waiter wags his tail. I drink double shots of Scotch, the day's pain rolling away, the day's fear blending into pleasure. The waiter lays our fortune cookies on the table and Beryl winks at him. He follows us to the door. She touches his arm and he wavers, wobbles, passes into bliss. "See you later, luv," Beryl grins. The poor man opens and closes his mouth, unable to produce sound.

The men urge me to quit high-rise construction. Sooner or later, they say, I'm going to get hurt, maybe even killed. Their hands are criss-crossed with jagged scars, missing thumbs and fingers.

"Junior," says Manny Rogers, one of the carpenters I work with, "lemme give you a piece of advice. Get your ass out of this business while it's still in one piece. See, nobody gives a shit about us. We're just fodder for the mill, that's all. A woodbutcher's life ain't worth shit up here. Ain't nothin' to look forward to 'cept gettin' laid off or killed. Not sure which one is worse, myself." Manny comes to work half drunk some mornings, and lots of the men drink on the job. The concrete floor of each completed deck is littered with beer cans and broken half pints of liquor. When we put up columns, one of the most dangerous jobs on high-rise, everyone jockeys for the inside, fearing that a drinker will stumble or tilt the column, knocking the rest of us over the side.

Johnny Lee pushes us to work harder and faster, telling us that Hillman Corporation has to meet its deadline, its shareholders need their dividend checks, the company's profit margins have to be kept high if we want to keep our jobs.

"Boys," he says, "if we don't top off by the end of August, we'll all be up a shitcreek without a paddle."

The men worry about getting maimed or killed, but are even more afraid of being laid off so they risk their lives. It doesn't matter how hard, or how little, one works. The layoffs are random and without warning. Shortly before the whistle blows to end work, Johnny walks the deck, his cowboy hat pulled down low, handing out pink slips. It is bad form to complain or ask why. Just pocket the slip, take what you're owed, and walk away.

"Don't act like that crybaby they laid off last week," says Manny Rogers. "Followed Johnny Lee around, beggin' to be kept on. Hell, you'd thought the sonbitch was a damn woman. Lay me off, I won't give those bastards the satisfaction."

The heat increases, tempers flare, threats are exchanged, mistakes are made. An old carpenter with a punching bag face and few teeth left in his scorched head comments about my hair, suggesting I look like a girl. "Why don't you go fuck yourself," I hiss, clutching my hammer so hard that my knuckles ache. He laughs and walks away. After two days of heavy rain, Manny cuts through the cord on his own skillsaw, dropping the live electrical wire into the ankle-deep water we're working in. He holds the saw aloft, giggling and pointing to its three-foot yellow tail.

"Goddamn, Junior," he sings, "almost fried us up for good that time didn't I."

A week later, the crane is laying a huge pile of steel on one corner of the deck when suddenly the men are cursing and running for the stairs, tossing away their tools in a mad scramble to escape. This time, the props hold and we're not hurled into space, but we work through the rest of the afternoon with our heads down, exchanging angry, embarrassed glances. No one jokes or even talks. When the whistle blows, the men pack up their tools and head for the stairs. Today, we outran death. We may have to do it again tomorrow.

"Seen it happen on another job," says Manny, giving me a lift into Washington. "Craneman dropped too much steel in one place. Concrete underneath was still wet. Deck just buckled. Men went flyin' out, flappin' and squawkin' like a chicken with his head off. Killed some of 'em deader'n hell. Left some of 'em cripples. Foreman'd been on our asses all summer. Push push push. Sonbitch went to the happy huntin' ground that day, and I was glad to see him go."

When the ambulance comes for someone on the next building over, no one on our site knows who got hurt.

"Might be the super's kid," Manny laughs. "Smart-ass fell down the elevator shaft one day. Ran a rod right up his ass. Served him right."

The ambulance crawls along the access road, kicking up dust. My stomach fills with hot soapy water. Johnny Lee screams for more plywood, the crane waves its proboscis, and miniature cars race back and forth on Jeff Davis Highway. I've nearly been killed three times on this job, slipping on a loose stringer and hanging out over the edge until Manny Rogers crawled out and pulled me back; starting to fly off the deck when the wind caught the plywood sheets I was carrying on my back, turning them into wings; miraculously escaping electrocution.

Shortly before the whistle blows on payday, Johnny walks around the deck, handing out little brown envelopes stuffed with crisp new money. Some of the men are already half drunk. Laborers and a few carpenters gather in the hole beneath our building to roll dice. "Come on baby, come to mama baby, come to me baby," they shout, tossing the bones across the mud-packed floor. The superintendent has luck. He squats across from the men, grinning and shaking his head in mock commiseration as he wins back their entire week's wages. When a laborer loses everything, the super advances him more cash. Some of the players are weeks in debt to the super. They keep rolling the dice.

The laborers work up to their knees in wet concrete, scooping it in huge shovels or smoothing it over with long boards, their faces inches from the surface, still shoveling and troweling when the whistle blows and the carpenters and their helpers leave for home. They pull down wooden forms when we move from floor to floor, working in closed-in areas, their bodies and lungs coated with dust. With one or two exceptions, the carpenters and their helpers are white, the laborers black.

"Hell no, I don't hate them people," Manny Rogers insists. "That's just what you people up north think. I go possum and coon huntin' with Jonsey all the time. Comes to my house. Just can't come in, that's all. My wife loves Jonsey too, just don't want him in the house. So he waits outside. Ain't no big thing. He don't mind. It's natural, Junior, that's what it is. Just the way things is, always have been, always gonna be that way."

"I've been down here too long," I tell Beryl. "The men say

I'm gonna wind up dead, mutilated, or paralyzed. What's the point? What would that prove? I've come so close to getting killed. Three times in just six months. Do you know what Manny Rogers said when I asked him why he does this kind of work? He said, 'Well, I tried coal minin' for a few years. Guess I just decided that twenty stories up was better'n twenty stories under.'

"I hate this fucking town. All these stupid artificial lines you're not supposed to cross. Whites live in Maryland, blacks live in 'Little Africa.' Whites make the laws, blacks are supposd to obey them. Keep quiet, work at shit jobs, go off to Vietnam and come back in a goddamn box. What kind of fucking nonsense is that? This town is just one huge plantation, Beryl. The slave owners live out in Virginia, and come to the capital to talk about what they're going to do about their uppity niggers. The biggest slave owner lives in the White House, just a few blocks from some of the poorest, sorriest-looking neighborhoods I've ever seen, places that make the Lower East Side look nice. You walk out at night and the cops tell you to get your ass off the streets. It's too dangerous to walk around the plantation after sundown. Too fucking dangerous to walk around the capital of the 'free world' Beryl. I don't see very many 'free' people here. Sometimes, it's hard to believe we're even living in the twentieth century. I really expect Rhett Butler to come riding down Pennsylvania Avenue with Scarlett O'Hara on the back of his horse.

"Besides, I really miss the Lower East Side. I miss Puerto Ricans. I miss hippies. I miss Zarro. I even miss junkies, Beryl. Siobhan wrote the other day. Said Windsong likes to look out the window and dance to the Supremes. Her first word was 'fuck.' And I wasn't even there to hear it."

"But I'm sick. What am I supposed to do? I need an operation," Beryl says. "You can't just leave me here."

"I'm going. I'll give Lucille a month's rent for the room. I'll leave you some money."

"You bloody bastard. How can you do this? I came down here just to be with you. You're just like every other man—a fucking coward." She starts to cry. "I don't know anyone here. I don't have a job. I left the hospital just to be with you."

"You'll get by, Beryl."

"How?"

"The same way you always have. You know you've been buying insurance with that Chinese waiter down the street."

"What do you mean? How can you say that?"

"He's been coming over here while I'm at work, and you know it."

"That's a lie."

"That's the truth. The landlady told me. Heard the old bed rattling. And you made a little Freudian slip last week. I found your diaphragm drying out in the bathroom."

"That was because you and I . . ."

"No, Beryl. We haven't had sex for three days, and you know it."

"Yes we did, just last night, didn't we?"

"No."

"Well, it's been in there since the last time, that's all."

"No, Beryl."

"I forgot, that's all. It's been inside me all this time."

"You never forget to take it out."

"Well, just this once I did. I came down here just to be with you and now . . ."

"You came down here because you needed a place to stay, Beryl. You got tired of dropping acid in Manhattan State. I had a job, some money. Well, I don't have a job anymore. I quit this afternoon. Told Johnny Lee I'm going home. He gave me the rest of my pay. I'm going back to the city."

"You just want to go back to that little bastard daughter of yours."

"My what?"

"You heard me."

"And what about the one you put up for adoption, Beryl? At least my daughter knows where I am."

"You're the cruelest person I've ever met. You're going to get what's coming to you. You're just like Oscar Wilde, a homo, a queer, a man who likes it in the ass, that's all you are."

"Why don't you think of something new to call me?"

"Go home and screw your mother. That's what your problem is. That's all you ever really wanted. I hope they do lock you up in the nuthouse where you belong, before you hurt anyone else. You are nuts, you know that don't you? All these years you've blamed your family, but I could tell them a thing or two. I ought to write them a letter. I ought to tell them who you really bloody are. The only mistake they ever made was letting you out of the bloody hospital. YOU ARE A MENTAL PATIENT. AND YOU ALWAYS WILL BE A MENTAL PATIENT."

"I'm not going back to Iowa, Beryl. I'm going back to our neighborhood."

"Just go, you sonofabitch. Just get out. I never loved you. I just told you that because I felt sorry for you. I thought maybe I could help you. Make you into a decent human being. Now I see that's not possible. You're a bastard, and you'll always be a bastard. You hate women, that's your problem. And you're too much of a coward to come out of the closet. You're a little fag, and you know it. At least Alfie has the guts to be queer. You keep up that front, drinking, fighting, fucking everything that walks. Mr. HE-MAN. But you don't fool anyone except yourself. Everyone on the Lower East Side knows about you. You claim you've been raped twice. HA, I'll wager you enjoyed it. You like it that way. You know you do. At least Oscar Wilde had class. You don't even have that. Now get out of here. Leave me alone. Let me have some peace."

"I'll see you back on the block, Beryl."

"No you won't, not this time you bloody won't. You'll never see me again. Not this time."

"Maybe you'll be speaking Chinese when I see you again."

"Get out of my life you dirty little bastard. Leave me to die in peace. You don't care what happens to me or to anyone else, including yourself. Go back to Alfie and get buggered. Your faggot friends will take you in. They love little boys like you. All you have to do is spread your legs . . ."

"You ought to know, Beryl."

"Get out before I start screaming. You're not a man," she sobs. "You'll never be a man. You don't have it. You just don't have it. You're a faggot, that's what you are. A faggot, not a man. A real man . . ."

I drop two hundred dollars on the bed, close the door, hoist my duffel bag and walk out to the sidewalk, hesitating,

half expecting Beryl to follow but when I look back there is
no one there.

Light reflects off his spit-shined shoes, his pants are ironed
into blades, and his head is a giant egg resting on the back
of the seat. His hands and feet are too small for his muscular
body and his lowslung jaw is filled with crooked little teeth.
He sleeps with his mouth open, muttering and sniffling. The
train is cool and comfortable, passengers sipping coffee,
reading the papers, chatting. Brooks Brothers' suits, Flors-
heim shoes, Parisian dresses, gold watches, diamond rings,
scented soaps, aftershave lotions. Copies of the *Atlantic, New
Yorker, Saturday Review, Washington Post, New York Times* spread
open on well-pressed laps.

I lean back in my chair, open the tattered paperback in
my lap, sip a Bloody Mary. My shoes are scuffed, pants wrinkled, all of my possessions stored at my feet. The Marine
snorts, opens his eyes.

"Where are we?" he asks.

"Delaware."

"Delaware?"

"Yeah."

"I been asleep long?"

"A couple of lifetimes."

He looks at me, squints, thrusts out his jaw.

"Where you going?" he demands.

"New York?"

"New York?"

"Yeah, I live there."

"What the hell for?"

"I like it."

"You like what?"

"The city. Where are you going?"

"Oh, I just got out of boot," he says, lighting a Lucky Strike,
holding out the pack.

"No thanks, I don't smoke. Out of a boot?" I say, looking
squarely into his handsome blue eyes.

"No, basic training," he says, removing a comb and running it along the sides of his nearly bald head. "Parris Island.

Six weeks a pure hell, but I'm ready now. Ready as I'll ever be."

"Ready?"

"For Nam, man. You haven't heard? There's a war goin' on."

"I heard, but . . ."

"You never been in the service?"

"Not really."

He looks at me as though I've offered him a cup of arsenic.

"No? How come?"

"I was in ROTC for two years, then got drafted in 1960, but . . ."

"Got drafted, but didn't have to go through basic?"

"No."

"Well, what the hell?"

"It's a long, long, story."

"Yeah, I'll bet," he says, lighting another cigarette and shifting toward the window.

"Do you really want to go to Vietnam?" I ask.

"Hell yes," he says.

"Why?"

"Why? Only a civilian would ask that kind a question. 'Why?' Jesus Christ, because the communists have to be stopped before they take over the world, that's why."

"But, what's goin' on?" I ask, picking up his slow, irritated way of speaking.

"Goin' on? I told you, a war's goin' on. Don't they sell newspapers up there in New York? Americans gettin' their asses shot off over there. Comin' home in body bags. Somebody's gotta stop that shit, and it might as well be the Marines. None of them other candy-assed people can do it. Navy's nothin' but a bunch a queers. Air Force is mama's boys too. Army'd be just like sendin' the Girl Scouts over there."

"Aren't you worried about getting killed?"

"Killed?" he says, blowing smoke toward the ceiling. "No way Jimmy Robins' gonna get wasted. Gonna kick ass and take names. Semper Fi, Marine. Know what that means? Hell no, civilians don't understand."

"Understand what?"

"The Corps. What it means to be in the crotch, part of the green machine."

"I've already been in a war," I say.

"What?" he demands. "How's that? What war you ever been in?"

"Not this war," I say. "My own private war."

"Man, New York's weird. Draft dodgers and queers. In the Corps, we'd bust their heads if them people acted like that."

I tell the Marine about an ambush in the Ia Drang Valley where hundreds of American soldiers were killed in one day. According to news accounts, clumps of wounded lay dying in the elephant grass, screaming for their girlfriends and their mothers while squads of North Vietnamese stalked them, executing them one by one.

"I've heard them stories," he says. "So what? They weren't Marines. Besides, I don't expect it to be no game of ping-pong. War's war, that's all. My great-great-granddad was in the Civil War. Granddad served in World War I. My own dad was in World War II. So was my uncle. My cousin is still MIA in Korea. So now it's my turn. Big deal. They're fuckin' with the wrong people over there. The army, well, they're just a bunch a pussies. Marines is different. Nobody bad enough in this world to kick our ass. Nobody. Not at Guadalcanal, not at Iwo Jima, Korea, not in Vietnam, not anywhere. Never happen."

"Well," I say, extending my hand when he gets up to leave the train at Trenton, "good luck to you, Marine."

"Thanks," he says. "I appreciate it." People leaving, boarding the train, the Marine unmoving, blocking the aisle, as though waiting for some command. The train gently rocking on its wheels and the Marine spinning, staring hard into my eyes for a moment. "Pray for me, will you?" I try to speak, but he's already walking—shoulders back, chest out, huge duffel bag over his right shoulder—along the platform. When he reaches the stairs he pauses, but no one rushes forward to greet him. The train lurches forward. He doesn't see me waving.

The train rolls down the ugly corridor between Trenton and New York, stopping at Princeton to pick up commuters with newspapers tucked under their arms, styrofoam cups in one hand, briefcases in the other. "You will sit on a train, martini in hand, newspaper on your lap, wondering why you feel so claustrophobic, so empty inside." Had Doctor Maynard put those books (Paul Goodman's *Growing Up Absurd,* James Baldwin's *Another Country,* Richard Wright's *Black Boy,* C. Wright Mills's *The Power Elite*) on the shelves in Clarion's library, knowing I would spend hours poring through each text, reverently turning each one over in my hands, as though just by touching them I could travel into some new and exciting and dangerous universe. I read and reread the works Dr. Maynard left (for me?), studying them like a student preparing for a life and death exam: Pass, and my release from Clarion would be assured. Fail, and I would remain in the snakepit forever.

At some intuitive level, I knew that Dr. Maynard was determined to shake all of my foundations loose. Yet like a drowning man who clutches at twigs, I held on to bits and pieces of my past, unable or unwilling to swim—as he was urging me to do—straight out to sea. Each time I wavered, insisting that I must spend a little more time on land, he would leave another life raft on which, should I choose to do so, I could drift further out to sea. I rode the waves, rising and falling, still fearing I might drown, always looking back, struggling to turn toward the deadly safety of land.

But the moorings did break loose, and finally I sailed off, crossing out of one decade, one universe, into another. Now, as the conductor calls out the last remaining stops before New York, I feel a certain detached excitement, not the kind I experienced years ago when the bus climbed over the Pulaski skyway, passing Jersey City, beginning its descent into the Lincoln Tunnel, not the loneliness as I stood bag in hand in front of Port Authority bus terminal, waiting for Neal Cassady or Jack Kerouac himself to beckon me into some battered old '55 Chevy filled with hipcats in shades and berets, jamming and snapping their fingers to Miles Davis as they passed a bottle of cheap port and a pipe filled with Algerian hash from mouth to mouth.

"Wow, man. You're alive. Like groovy," Zarro sings, spotting me in Tompkins Square Park. "I mean, I can't believe my

eyes. Far fucking out, man. You're not dead. Heard you'd
gone down, man. Flying squirrel trip in front of the IRT.
Said people saw your soul floatin' in a gondola down the East
River. Said the Gestapo barbecued your lobes up in Bell-a-
vue. Like dig it, man. I kid you not. I got the news. Left,
right. Up, down. Back, forward. Man, the lampposts were
whisperin', the streets loud jivin', even those fatass pigeons
tellin' tales. Heard you and Julie Trees had words with the
man and he wasted you BAM BAM BAM. And your bones
groovin' out on pauper's island. Just thrown in a hole, man,
like they do to us poets in this land of merry hate.

"Said said said said. But I knew you'd show man. I said,
'Man's hip to what's happenin', ain't nobody gonna take him
down. He's a survivor. He'll show.' Like Jesus takin' the nails
outa his own hands, man, pullin' them loose from the cross,
steppin' down, chompin' on that crown of thorns as though
it were a donut, man. Two bites and it's gone. And the Beatles
man. You know, like 'All ya need is love, love, all ya really
need is love' and J.C. twisting on the Red Sea, you dig. You
understand, the man just walks out there, walks out onto the
water, and this little boat comes by with Ringo playin' the
drums, John hittin' the guitar, and there it is, the son of God
dancing on the waves, groovin' to the sounds of them little
punks from Liverpool. Wow, man. I could dig it. I really
could."

"What's happening?" I say, shaking Zarro's grubby hand.

"I'll tell you what, man. This is what," Zarro says, pro-
ducing a book from inside the waist of his saggy flower-print
pants. "This is what's happenin', the latest *thing,* my man."

"What is it, Zarro?"

"What is it? You're not hip to Tolkien, man? This, my man,
is *the book. The book of life,* man. It's hobbits. Little people.
Merry folk. Hobbits. Where it's at, man. You don't know?
Where you been? I mean . . ."

"No, Zarro. Where do they live?"

"Where do they live? Where do they live? You're lookin' at
one, that's where they live. I, Zarro, am a Hobbit. You dig?"

"I'm not sure."

"Look here, man," Zarro cries, dancing in little circles and
waving the book. "Hobbits got their shit together. Kind of
like beats, man. Kind of like us, only better man. They just

hang out. Facto. Eat, drink, smoke dope in their little pipes, sing, tell stories, ball whenever they feel like it, sleep. Man, I tell you. This book transcends, man. It breaks through. It rolls you back. It takes you forward. It bounces you on its lap. Facto. Fucks with your mind. Pries you loose. It jolts your joint. It fries your fritters. It sucks your eyes right out of your head. Oh, man, this is better than Ginsberg. Better than Burroughs. Better'n any of them cats. Them dudes are still stalking on the wrong time zone, still prancing through the land puke, you dig?

"Really, now, hear what I'm sayin'. Can you? Facto, don't I know, listen to the wind blow, let it go. I can't loan you my copy, man, cause it's like my Bible now. I carry it with me everywhere, even when I'm ballin' some chick. I just take it out and lie it right by my side, because it provides the aura, the right light, purifies the air, cleans out the bad vibes, burns away the nasty brush, offers the mood, makes us come like rhinos, wall-shakin' ballin', man, window-breakin' screwin', screamin' so loud the subways stop, make the Empire building sway, drop the Brooklyn Bridge right into the bay."

"Hobbits do all that, Zarro?"

"FACTTTTTTTOROYALA, man. Like I say. Another range, that's all. I can't really explain. It's not words. Words don't work anymore. We got to get beyond words, man. I mean you can write all the poetry you want. You people over at La Mama and Le Metro can scream yourself hoarse, man. But it's still words. I'ts time to think up somethin' new. Somethin' that really says where it's at. And words just can't do it."

"But why not, Zarro? Isn't that a book?"

"This?" he cries, waving *The Hobbit* over his head. "No, man. I'm trying to tell you. This is no book. This is another world. This is *the* word. This is new age. This is what's comin'. This is 'Somethin' is happenin' but you don't know what it is, do you Mister Jones?' Dylan's been tellin' us, man. Now it's here. And if you miss it, you've missed it all, man. I mean, you might as well be Rip Van Winkle. Go to sleep and the world's like this," he said, waving his arms about the park. "Wake up and we're in the shire, man. We're gonna change it. But not through words. Through being kind, man. Through lovin'. Through layin' back, like brother Bilbo, you dig? Read the book, man. Join us, man. Like, be a hobbit."

Rice and beans, cuchifritos, Spanish music blasting from windows and doorways, junkies nodding in the park, dogs squatting on the sidewalk, cops cruising by, scoping hippie chicks with their tight little bottoms squeezed into Levis or miniskirts, cloudfluffy hair, Snow White skin, working on a badass wiggle but the cops only laugh at them and wave. I walk uptown on Avenue B, listening to the blues sounds and smelling the barbecue aromas that float through open doors and windows of the new "Soul Food" restaurants. A man in a flowery shirt, shades, his head shaved even cleaner than the Marine I met on the train, stands in the doorway, watching me move. I am deeply tanned, hard-muscled, summer blond, my hands cut up and scarred from working high-rise. I stop, shift my shopping bag to my left shoulder, hold his stare.

"What you lookin' at motherfucker?" he says.

"What?" I say, casually setting my bag down on the sidewalk. From inside the restaurant a woman's voice is calling.

"Come way from there now, goddamn it. We don't need no trouble today, Mulford. Got enough problems tryin' to pay bills. Don't need the man on our ass today. Get your black ass inside here, NOW, Mulford."

"I'm lookin' at you, that's what," I reply, moving closer to the man in the doorway, hands out of my pockets, casually down at my sides. Without hair, his head looks rounder and much bigger than it was five years ago. His hands are puffy, his stomach large, a nasty-looking goatee hangs from his chin He looks twenty, not just five years older.

"Cool it, man," I say, smiling. "I just want to ask you something. Listen. I want to ask . . ."

"Say what? I didn't invite you into my house, did I? What you want to ask, boy? I ain't talkin' to your white ass, so move it on down the street."

"I thought I heard that woman say . . ."

"What the fuck you talkin' about my woman for? What you

want here anyway? You want to eat, go ahead and eat. This is her place. I can't stop you. She'll take your money."

"Mulford? Did she say 'Mulford'? Is that what she said?"

The man in the doorway takes a step backward, puts his right hand in his pocket and holds it there.

"Who's askin'?" he whispers. "Who you with anyway, motherfucker?"

"Get your hand out of your pocket man. I'm not with anybody. Do I look like a cop? Take it easy, man. Calm down. Open your eyes. It's me, man. Me. Don't you remember me?"

"Goddamn, man, what's in it for you?"

"Don't you know me, Mulford? Don't you remember?"

"Know you? Why should I *know* you? All white people look alike to me," he chuckles.

"Listen, Mulford, I'll tell you why. Listen to this."

> *White man, you smother me with oppression*
> *Then lock me up for your aggression,*
> *You kill my people's dreams*
> *With your vicious racist things.*

The figure in the doorway frowns and shakes his head.

"No, man. Not 'things.' It goes like 'schemes,' man. You kill my people's dreams, with your vicious racist *schemes*. But how the hell?" He takes his hand out of his pocket, replaces his shades with a pair of gold-rimmed bifocals, squints, nods, steps onto the sidewalk.

"Man, I'm trying . . ."

"It's me, Mulford. Remember? Clarion. The snake pit. Des Moines, Iowa. When they let me out of Clarion I bought a one-way bus ticket heading east. *The Clarion Review.* Fat Man. Sissy. Frog Lady. They were keeping you in a room off by yourself, off in the quarantine ward, and the orderlies would bring me over to visit you. We'd drink instant coffee, talk, argue, read our poems aloud. We'd talk about James Baldwin's novel, *Another Country*, you'd get mad at me, call me a no good whitebread motherfucker, say those 'niggers' who stabbed and tried to kill me when I was fifteen turned my brain to fried mush. You'd go on and on. 'You ain't never gonna be black, whitebread, so give up tryin'. Stop readin' our books. Stop listenin' to our music. Stop fuckin' our women. You're just nothin' but a lame-assed slave owner like the rest, so don't be jivin' me about being black.' Remember, Mulford? Then you'd kick me out, but a couple of days later you'd send a note over to my ward, asking me to come and visit you soon. When I came back you'd greet me with, 'Say now, whitebread, where you been, anyway?'"

"Oh man," he sighs, blinking and shaking his head. "I can't believe it, man. I mean, damn, I thought you'd be dead by now."

Mulford shuffles forward, holding out his hand, looking old and happy.

"You lookin' different," he says, almost smiling. "Bad, real bad, man. Like you ready to take on the world. Damn, and me just about to go upside your head."

"Good thing for your sake you didn't try, Mulford," I laugh, taking his hand in mine.

"Tried? Mulford don't *try* nothin'. He just *does*, that's all."

"Mulford?"

"Yeah, man. Been a long time. A long, long time. Well come on in here. Meet my old lady. Sit down, man. You hungry? I remember you did love barbecue."

"Still do, Mulford."

"Well," Mulford calls into the kitchen, "how about bringin' this man out some food, baby?"

"Mulford," the woman warns, "I said no fightin' now. I'm tryin' to run a business, but you keep drivin' all the customers away."

"We're not fightin' babe. This is my man, from Iowa. We done some time together. Locked both our asses up in the nuthouse, but here we are, man. Here we are."

The woman brings a plate of barbecued pork and steamed collard greens.

"This here's my main woman. Calls herself Honeybee," Mulford says. "Up here from Birmingham. Know where that is? Badass town, that's where. You tired a livin', go down to Alabama. They'll take care of your white ass in a minute. Honeybee, this is my friend. Grew up in the same place I did. Well, not exactly. Same city, not the same neighborhood. Even in the north we couldn't do that. Still can't. Probably never will. Man's a poet, Honeybee. Writes fine stuff. Used to, anyway. I quit writin' a long time ago. Couldn't do much a that in the joint."

"They put you in prison, Mulford?"

"Hell yes, don't you remember? Caught me with a mother-fuckin' joint wrapped up in my nappy-ass hair. Thought I had it hidden real good. But when the man grabbed me, it fell out. Five years, for one stick. That's white man's justice. Got it down to two and a half with a bargain. Did two, split."

"Escaped?"

"No, they let my ass out on parole and I just walked, that's all. Picked up what I had, which wasn't much, and crossed the state line. Wasn't goin' back to no joint."

"Man, Mulford, you've changed a lot. You're . . ."

"Bigger? Yeah, man, I gained thirty pounds in the joint. Had to. First day in motherfucker looks at me, 'Mulford, that's a girl's name ain't it?' he says. I says, 'Girl's name?' Who you callin' a girl?' I kicked that nigger in the mouth, put my foot right down his teeth. Hell, man, I didn't want no trouble. But the man wasn't goin' to make me his punk. Not then, not ever. When he dropped I jumped right on his face, him lying out on the floor moanin' like a stuck pig and me standin' on his head. 'I'm gonna be in the joint for a long fuckin' time,' I told him. 'And when I see your sorry ass I'm gonna put my foot up it, you dig? So motherfucker you don't go talkin' about my name, hear?'"

Mulford laughs, sips from a can of Ballantine, adjusts his shades.

"Man, I didn't even know where the fuck I was. But after that I started pumpin' iron, doing sit-ups, push-ups, shadow boxin', everything I could to get bigger. I ate all the poison they fed us, scoffed up all the grease man. 'Cause I wanted to grow. And I did, man. Got to be one of the biggest cats on that block. Guards were all pigs. Never seen a black man before until they come to work in the joint. Some of the brothers were Muslims. You know, tryin' to get away from the white devil. I'm sorry, man, but you don't understand. I mean, you can try, but you can't."

"Yeah, Mulford, I suppose you're right."

"I'm not just talkin' about the color of your skin, brother.

That's not the thing. It's a sickness we're talkin' about. Somethin' you people been handin' down from generation to generation, man. Somethin' you just can't help cause it's in your blood, your bones. See, problem is you come from a long line of devils, man. A long, long line."

"Could be, Mulford, but I can't change my color any more than you can. We're stuck inside our skin I guess."

"Yeah, my man Malcolm was comin' round to that."

"And some of his own brothers killed him."

"Listen here now," Mulford says, pounding his fist on the table. "Muslims didn't kill Malcolm. The CIA did, cause Malcolm was talkin' about violations of human rights. Not in some jive communist country, but right here man, right here in the U.S.A. Do you know he was plannin' to tell the United Nations about it? Gonna tell them how the man won't rent to us, won't hire us for jobs, how white people want to turn our women into whores, our kids into junkies, our lives into a living hell.

"Malcolm was gonna tell them how the pigs insult and beat us when they take us down, the way they stick their guns against your eyeball, cock the hammer and twirl the chamber, laughing when we piss in our pants, the way they smack us on the ass and back and head, places where it won't show, callin' us niggers and jigaboos and coons, all kinds a shit like that. Malcolm just wanted to tell the world what the white devil's been doin' to us for the last two hundred years, and how he's still gettin' away with it.

"So the CIA knocked him off, but that don't mean he's not talkin'. You mark it down, baby, Malcolm X is alive, and he's gonna stay alive as long as you people keep fuckin' with us. The guards were celebratin', laughin'. 'Your man X got what was comin' to him,' that's what they said. 'Just like you're gonna get what's comin' to you, pig,' only I didn't say it out loud. Wasn't ready to die, not even for Brother Malcolm."

"Are you a Muslim, Mulford?"

"No man, I tried for a while. Didn't eat swine, didn't touch alcohol or drugs for a long time, but I'm weak. No discipline. Just couldn't keep away from women and booze."

"What's gonna happen, Mulford?"

"Hell, I don't know. I'm just takin' it day by day, man. You

133

know, waitin' for things to burn. And they will, man. Oh, baby they will. Watts's already gone, right down to the ground. They'll be more. Sooner or later this city's gonna go up in smoke. Sooner or fuckin' later. Whole country's gonna burn, man. Right down to the ground."

"So you and I are gonna be shootin' it out? That's what it comes down to, Mulford?"

"Oh hell no, baby," he laughs. "Not you. I'll leave you be. You're cool. Just stay home when you hear the shootin' start, that's all. Keep out of sight. Pull down the shades. Lock your doors. Take your woman to bed. Wait for things to cool out."

"I don't have a home, Mulford."

"No home?"

"No, I just move around. Here, there, everywhere. People's floors, furnished rooms, the streets. Still a beatnik, Mulford."

"A beatnik? Oh yeah," Mulford laughs. "I remember. But the streets are a bad scene, whitebread."

"Not really. I've gotten used to it. I don't like being tied down."

"Yeah, man. I can dig it.

"I feel safer in the streets than in most apartments."

"Yeah, man. I can understand that. My old lady keeps tryin' to get me to work, but I just say, 'Baby, life's work enough, why look for trouble?' I'm waitin', that's all, just waitin' to see what goes down."

"Me too, Mulford, like *Waiting For Godot.* "

"Oh yeah, man. Story of my whole fucking life. Waiting for somethin', somewhere, waitin'."

I tell Mulford about Sean McBride, an alcoholic acting student who let me sleep on his couch for a few weeks. Sean worked uptown for a psychiatrist who liked Puerto Rican boys, kept several three-hundred-pound prostitutes in his apartment, collected pornography, and ran a flower shop that specialized in ripping off rich Upper East Side ladies. The psychiatrist let Sean take patients' charts home, and Sean liked to read them aloud to his friends, who thought them terribly funny.

"Patient: 'So I do feel guilty, because I masturbated our pet Beagle for three years. Yes, sometimes I performed oral sex on him too. And once I even tried ...' (Patient pauses here.) 'even tried . . .' (Patient can't continue. Weeps. Shows signs of deep-seated guilt. I offer sedation. Suggest lithium.)"

On and on Sean would read. On and on his friends would laugh. Sean seldom kept food in the apartment, and the coyote wouldn't leave me alone, chewing away at my insides until I grew quite weak from hunger and started sleeping a lot, dreaming always of food, eating every scrap of stale bread, mushy crackers, ancient jars of gelfilte fish, even the rug if I could have figured out how to cut it up and cook it. Sean announced that he was having a party, and that James Baldwin would be there, but I just thought he was drunk again, or dreaming his own fame and fortune.

"The apartment was packed elbow to elbow, nose to nose. Most of the guests were women, and Sean had laid up a great store of liquor and marijuana for the occasion. By nine o'clock many of the guests were drunk or stoned and a young woman from Wisconsin, blue eyes, deep red hair, was leaning against the refrigerator, telling Sean about the time her roommate was mugged and beaten on her way home from a party in the West Village and Sean's laughter seemed to inspire the storyteller, who offered even more graphic details, describing the crime as though it were the Grand Prix. "Then she . . . Then he . . . Then he." Sean was laughing uncontrollably. "Then she . . ." Sean was coughing and spitting and the door to his apartment swung open knocking one young drunk in the head as a stentorian soprano announced:

"LADIES AND GENTLEMEN, MAY I PRESENT TO YOU . . . MR. JAMES BALDWIN.

"The room fell into a hush, rising slowly to a giggle, and suddenly the crowd was shoving and pushing to see or touch Sean's guest, whose companion kept shouting that everyone would have a chance to say hello but that time was limited and people should stop pushing. Sean was trying to get through the crush but no one budged so he pushed harder and someone pushed back and Sean punched him in the face and Jimmy's companion elbowed a path into the next room where I was standing. He told me that I had exactly two minutes to speak with the author and I started to tell Baldwin about finding *Another Country* on the shelves of a remarkable library in a snakepit in southern Iowa. I was tell-

ing Jimmy how a black kid named Mulford and I read passages from his work aloud, how much I admired him, and
that it was a great honor . . . but the companion gave me a
slight "time's up" shove with the tips of his fingers and I
started screaming that he'd better keep his fucking hands off
me unless he wanted his ass kicked and that I'd talk to Jimmy
as long as I goddamn felt like it, or longer, and more people
were trying to squeeze through the door but Sean slammed
it on a young woman's hand and her boyfriend tried to throw
a punch but was caught midair between the shoving crowd,
and the companion was shouting that everyone must take
turns and Jimmy was smiling, listening, talking softly and
graciously to everyone and I got pushed into a corner and
into an argument with a woman I had once wrestled naked
through the night, telling her that Jimmy was homely and
that I was beautiful—even though the coyote had turned my
ribcage inside out and my eyes were floating deep and
gloomy inside their sockets—demanding to know why she
wanted to sleep with him, knowing he was gay, and that I was
terrific in bed, and she looked directly into my shabby little
ego and replied:

"Because Jimmy is famous and you're not, that's why."

"I woke alone in the dark on the couch, without Margie
(the starstruck wrestler), staggered into the hallway, my bare
feet sticking to a plaster of spilled beer and smashed pretzels,
and down the hall to the lavatory where I clutched the chain
we used to flush the toilet, trying to keep from falling head-
first into the bowl, and when I paddled back to Sean's door
it was bolted tight. I could hear him laughing and a woman's
giggle and then only silence, so I walked barefoot along Avenue B and sat in the park until the sun came up, feeling
happy because I had met James Baldwin, a privilege I
thought I would never have."

"You blew it, whitebread," Mulford laughs.

"Yeah, Mulford, I blew it."

"Got into a fight?"

"Yeah."

"Well, at least you got to see my man up close."

"For a couple of minutes, Mulford."

"*The Fire Next Time. Nobody Knows My Name.* Voice of the people, whitebread."

"Yeah, I think so Mulford."

"Man, you should have gone up side his head."

"Baldwin's?"

"Hell no, the white boy that was with him."

"No shit, Mulford. Next time I will. I'm sorry to hear they put you in the joint, man."

"Oh the joint's bad all right, but it ain't no different than the outside in a lot of ways. Just a matter of degree, whitebread. Man knocks our heads on the outside, knocks them on the fuckin' inside too. No big change. And Mulford needed it, man. Had to find out how the man really thinks. How things really go down. Always kinda believed I might be a little bit white. You know, that I could walk on the black *and* white side, you dig? I wanted a piece of both worlds, cause I wasn't ready to be what I was—a black man, an African, a proud motherfuckin' nigger. You understand? You dig? No, man. Probably not.

"The man understands one thing, and one thing only. The man understands violence. Here in New York, in Des Moines, in Selma, L.A., Detroit, Newark, Vietnam. All the same, man. Violence talks, bullshit walks.

"We tried to love the man, and what'd he do? Beat us up, put our asses in jail, killed our leaders. King just can't seem to get what Malcolm was sayin', cause Malcolm was talking about the jails, man. Talking about Harlem. Talking about the *real* America, not some make believe place called the 'melting pot.'

"I don't want any part of the white world, not anymore. I just want to be left alone. I want the man to stay out of my face, to keep his motherfuckin' hands out of my pockets, and off my women. You don't have to love me. You don't even have to like me. Just leave me ALONE, brother, that's all I ask. And I'll leave you be. From now until forever, man. You leave my ass alone, I'll leave yours."

"We go way back, Mulford."

"Yeah, man, we do, but I can't go makin' exceptions. I just got to live by what I know."

"I understand, man. We all do. Sometimes I wish I didn't

know what I know. Sometimes I'm ashamed to be white, Mulford." "Yeah, man, but you are what you are, dig? You ain't black.

You ain't never gonna be black, you dig?"

"Yeah, Mulford, I dig. Hope to see you around. Maybe rap some more."

"I'll be around, baby. Don't worry about that. Mulford's goin' hang in there. Like I say, man. They killed Malcolm, but it didn't do no good. We're not gonna forget him. Not now. Not ever. Malcolm changed everything, man, and I do mean permanent, forever. Man was a prophet. Sent here by God to tell it like it is. White people might not be listenin', but black folk ain't never gonna forget what he had to say. Listen, brother. You need some cash? I got a little extra."

"No, Mulford, I'm alright."

"Listen, man," Mulford grins, holding out a twenty dollar bill, "I haven't forgotten. Those cookies you used to bring me. And books. You got heart, brother. It ain't your fault you're white. Come on now. Take this. Buy your old lady somethin' nice. Know what I mean?"

"I'll do that, Mulford," I say, stuffing the bill into my pocket.

"Take care a your skinny white ass," he laughs.

"You too, Mulford. Stay out of the joint, man."

"Yeah, baby. Keep the faith."

Familiar sounds, familiar aromas, walking to familiar rhythms, I want to climb onto the bar and sing great praises to this neighborhood—thanking the Vazac for setting out its daily free lunch of boiled potatoes, raw fish, cucumbers, onions, and chunks of stale cheese, for its basket of boiled eggs, its twenty-five-cent ham sandwiches, and for the silver-haired bartender who tries to sell me handguns, lifting a napkin from a plate and saying, "Now take this little baby here, .25 caliber, strong enough knock a guy on his ass. You like it?" When I refuse, he just laughs, shakes his head, puts the gun back under the counter, and tells me another story about someone he knows who's been robbed (all his kin own liquor stores). Then he buys me another drink. Thanking Milly and Harold for great heaping plates of free greasy French fries, for giving struggling artists and writers credit, for their genuine love of art, for their love of Alfie, for their bimonthly "grand openings"—two straight hours of free food and booze. Thanking Ellen Stewart, owner of the La Mama Cafe, for allowing John and me, and so many of our friends, to read our poetry there. Thanking Ed Saunders for opening his Peace Eye bookstore, and the diggers for starting their storefront free clothing store, and all the "I fuck you, you fuck me" poets who hold forth at Le Metro cafe. Thanking Siobhan for offering to take me to pay homage to Woody Guthrie when he was dying in a New York hospital (I'd never heard of him), for dragging me into Gerde's Folk City to hear Dave Von Ronk, Buffy St. Marie, and other people she called "folk singers" (no charge if we stood behind a little barrier), for showing me the ways of the streets, for giving birth to Windsong when several psychiatrists tried to talk her out of being a mother. Thanking Julie Trees for wrapping her skinny legs around my back and riding me into the future, for showing me the underground railway to junkie crash pads, and for crushing my nostalgia beneath her existential heel. Thanking Stanley for this beatbar on Avenue B and 12th where many a winter night I've climbed out of the cold to nurse a mug of beer till my hands turned human again, trading blarney for booze, drinking and talking with writers and artists, and one night Jack Kerouac did show up, accompanied by a drunken entourage, and Stanley ordered him out of his bar and there was great keening as the crowd heaved to and fro, Stanley screaming that no one caused trouble in his bar, no one came in and fucked up his scene, and the keeners crying for the master to remain but the wailing having no effect on the street-tough Polish pub owner who pushed his own beergut into the surging crowd, building the tidal wave that swept Jack and pals out onto the sidewalk while the keening went on and on and Stanley shouting himself hoarse because he didn't care who it was IT COULD BE GOD, IT COULD BE JESUS, IT COULD BE THE PRESIDENT OF THE UNITED STATES, It could be ANYONE but NO ... BODY ... caused trouble in his place because the cops would come down on his head and lock his doors and then where would all the keeners go just because one loudmouth sonofabitch wanted to come in and cause trouble and . . .

The afternoon fades into cocktail hour and I continue drinking shots with beer chasers but the euphoria turns to sadness, like a host who prepares a sumptuous repast—pâté, steamed clams, stuffed artichokes, filet mignon, lobster tail, pheasant—a grand display of hospitality, and then the clock starts ticking off the hours and the guests are not arriving; the steamed clams turn into blobs of mucus, the filet mignon are malignant tumors floating in their gravy, the lobster tails resemble huge humpbacked slugs, the clock tick tick ticking while the host, weeping into his loneliness, creates gothic endings—perhaps a splash of gasoline on the Persian carpets, a glass of champagne while the fire roars and he pounds the piano and they will find his ashes, those dear friends who acted with such barbaric cruelty.

A woman at the far end of the bar, her hair expensively groomed, a pair of black tights stretched over her country club legs, the bartender pouring Chivas Regal over the ice in her glass; she is laughing and waving a cigarette and I keep looking at her but she refuses to respond and I edge closer, the Holden Caulfield she is with smiling at me as though I'm the funny new doorman from Dooo-bleen and:

"What's so funny?" I demand.

Caulfield looks annoyed.

"Why don't we go home?" I ask the woman.

"What?" Caulfield demands.

"Why don't you kiss my ass."

"What did you say?"

"Fuck you," I hiss.

"Maybe you'd like to talk about it outside," he says.

"Maybe I would."

"Todd," the woman says, "leave him alone, man, he's drunk."

"Can I buy you a drink?" Todd asks.

"Sure, after I kick your ass."

"Todd," the woman pleads, "fighting's just not cool, man. This isn't cool."

"Fighting's not cool," I mimic, heading for the door.

Holden and I walk out to the sidewalk and he starts to

140

speak but I hit him three times, expecting him to fall. Instead I am sitting on the sidewalk, blood dripping onto my chin, lips split, running my tongue over a chipped tooth. Outside my pain, I think how clever Holden is, how superfast, faster than my idol the former Cassius Clay, now Muhammad Ali, because I didn't even see the punch. I want to shake his hand, congratulate him, buy him and his lady friend a round of drinks, tell some stories, perhaps spend the night with them in their Bleecker Street pad. But then I hear the voice, see gold buttons on a blue tunic, the nightstick the cop must have swung round in front of my face, grasping it with both hands and yanking me backward, knocking me to the concrete.

"Get the fuck up, asshole," the cop says.

I stand up, spitting blood and a piece of tooth onto the sidewalk.

"Who the fuck do you think you are, Joe Louis?"

I stare at him.

"I asked you a fuckin' question."

I say nothing.

"O.K., bigshot, take a hike, and don't let me catch you around here again tonight, cause if I do I'm gonna break your fuckin' head, understand?"

Siobhan opens the door, wearing a ragged nightgown and smelling like newspapers left too long in the garbage. Puppy leaps forward, wrapping his huge paws around my neck, licking my cheeks and forehead with his rough tongue. I stumble backward, laughing, rolling on the floor with my dogfriend.

"Where have you been?" Siobhan demands. "You said you'd be here by noon. I made lunch. Windsong cried. She wanted to see her daddy. You're drunk. You're always drunk. I heard Beryl was living with you. You lied. You said she was in Manhattan State. We got the money you sent. I made Windsong a dress. She won't wear anything else. She likes to dance. She stands by the window, dancing and yelling "fuck." That was her first word. You missed it. You've got blood on your mouth. Fighting again. I'm leaving. I don't want Windsong to grow up here. Too many junkies. Too many rats. Too many crazies. Where is that bitch?" Siobhan demands.

"Washington. I left her there."

"So you were living together?"

"Not really."

"Sleeping in the same bed."

"Yeah."

"You lied."

"Yeah."

"You always lie."

"Not always. Stop looking. She isn't out there. She's in D.C., probably curled up beside her Chinese friend."

"Chinese?"

"Never mind."

"I'm leaving."

"Where are you going?"

"Out to the country."

"What country?"

"Not another country. Bucks County. Pennsylvania. I want to smell the honeysuckle again. I want to wade in a stream, hear the birds sing, watch the leaves turn colors, go swimming in a creek."

"Oh."

"Where there's green grass, birds, streams, flowers. Where Windsong can run and play."

"She can run and play in the park."

"There's too much dogshit in the park."

"There's enough of that in here."

"You don't have to come in. Sleep out on the street. I don't care."

"I don't have anyplace to go, Siobhan. I've got money in my pocket, don't want to get rolled. Here, I brought you some groceries."

"Then talk quietly. I just got her to sleep."

I tiptoe into the apartment, trying to avoid piles of clothes, books, foodcrusted plates, soggy diapers. Shadows zigzag round my shoes, popping softly when I step on them. The child, wearing only a pair of green shorts, is sleeping in a long wicker basket. Siobhan has the windows open, but it does no good. Puppy lies beside the basket, chest heaving, water dripping from his tongue. Heat funnels out of the sidewalks, climbing the fire escape, pouring through Siobhan's windows, filling the two tiny rooms. I lean down to kiss Windsong on the cheek, beads of sweat dripping from my forehead onto her stomach. I lift her in my arms, turn the long wicker basket over and tap it twice, the floor spinning black with cockroaches racing toward cracks in the plaster, climbing the walls, clinging to the ceiling, gumballs squishing under my boots.

A roach is stuck in the wall, legs frantically waving, huge eggsack dragging her down, preventing escape. I watch her struggle, trying to understand what makes these gruesome little creatures so tenacious, why they desperately want to live, why—like the junkies, the slumlords, the welfare department, the city of New York—they seem so determined to drive the tenants from these buildings. The slumlord promises to send in an exterminator but he never does. And even if he had, the roaches would return, dropping from the ceiling into bowls of soup, floating bellyup in the bathtub, swimming in the dishwater, mixing into spaghetti sauce, frying with the eggs, expanding the stroganoff Siobhan creates out of canned bullybeef the Welfare department distributes once a month.

I crush the pregnant roach into the wall with my palm, enjoying the soft little squishsound, feeling a strange rush, an almost heroic sense of triumph, as though by killing one fat prehistoric insect I can rescue my daughter from poverty and pain. I want to put Windsong on my back and flap my wings, rising high over Manhattan, soaring out over the Hudson River, breaking through the clouds and flying on until we reach the Rockies, a mountain stream, a meadow filled with spring flowers, rabbits nibbling new grass, goats kicking up their heels, fawns snuggling beside their mothers, no cars, no trucks, no drugs, no guns, no human beings.

I tell Siobhan about the Marine I sat next to on the train and the hobbit I met in the park. I talk about meeting Mulford on Avenue B, and how the cop knocked me to the sidewalk, splitting my lips and breaking my tooth. "Mulford says America's gonna burn. Burn to the ground. Says the white man is the devil. Says we're gonna pay. I sure hope so." Streetlight rippling across our naked bodies. Siobhan's breasts little anchored sailboats rising, falling. The sheets damp with sweat, sticky from our lovemaking.

"Siobhan . . ." I whisper. ". . . Hobbits . . . Siobhan . . . Vietnam . . . Siobhan . . . Mulford . . . Malcolm X . . . Wars . . . All kinds of wars. Men."

I dress quickly, kiss Windsong on the forehead and ease quietly out the door, out of this stifling rat and roach-infested tenement. The moon is up, sirens wailing, fireworks or gunfire in the distance. I walk the streets, waiting for some challenge, some word or fist, glint of blade or gun, adrenalin popping behind my eyes, driving down the cords in my arms and legs, my body gliding a step or two above the sidewalk. No crickets, hoot owls, or serenading frogs. Rats rattling garbage lids; junkies nodding and scratching; insomniacs hanging on the stoop; boys pumping their girlfriends in the stairwells; sweet smell of pot; sweet sound of Sonny Rollins blowing off a rooftop; someone weeping; someone screaming motherfucker.

I have no home; good to be home.

Clarion, Iowa, late December, '62.

"Listen," said Dr. Maynard, "I know you've been thinking about escaping from here, but please don't try it. You'll be out of here soon enough."

"What do you mean?"

"I mean I'm signing your release forms in a few days."

"You mean I can leave?"

"Yes."

"Now?"

"If you want to. But I hope you'll wait just a little longer. What are your plans?"

"Plans?"

"I mean after you leave here."

"Go home, I guess."

"Have you really thought about that?"

"No."

"I mean, what that means."

"Do you want me to stay here?"

144

"Hell no," said Dr. Maynard, blushing with anger. "You never belonged in here in the first place. That moron in Fairlawns keeps sending people down here, and we've got one doctor for every five hundred patients. One. How the hell . . . Oh, pardon me. I just meant to say that I know it's been rough for you. That I think you should . . . that you ought to . . . get away from everything. From your family . . . from," waving his hands, "this."

"I intend to."

"No, no. I don't think you really understand what I'm saying. I mean you're trapped. You're family's trapped. And nobody's going to win. So far, you're the biggest loser, but there are no winners in this game."

"But where should I go?"

"I'm not telling you to go anywhere. Just that you have to break this cycle if you don't want to spend the rest of your life in places like this. You've seen the pattern, haven't you? People leave here, and in a few months, or even weeks, they're right back. They're caught up in the revolving door. Spinning in and out of psychiatric hospitals, year after year."

"I don't have any money. Dropped out of college. I . . ."

Dr. Maynard shook a cigarette from his pack, offered me one, lighted mine and then his own. I was having difficulty lifting my arms, my knees were filling with warm water, and my chest ached. Dr. Maynard stared at me through a pair of thick tortoise-shell glasses. He smoked and said nothing. I knew he'd been in the joint for performing an abortion, that he'd lost his license to practice medicine and was paroled to work here, in the snakepit. The first time we talked I pounded my fist on the table, screaming that my family was trying to kill me, that he should bring my mother to Clarion, give her tests, shave her head, put her in prison clothes, run electricity through her brain.

I told him about falling in love after my first year in college. Meghan was petite, blond, blue-eyed, the perfect little homecoming queen, and the first time she took off her clothes I was lost. She told me she was a virgin and I believed her, and she said she had never been in love before and I believed that too. I worked all summer digging ditches in tropical heat and at night Meghan and I would lie together on a golf course, drinking beer, watching the stars, dreaming about our future. We said our souls were meeting, not just our bodies, and after making love we wrapped together on the soft summer grass, drifting in and out of sleep, promising this would be forever. She said she loved my mind, my body, my poetry, and then one day, without warning and with few words, she handed back my engagement ring. She'd met an Air Force pilot and, said Meghan, he was just more interesting.

"And that's why you cut your wrists?" Dr. Maynard asked.

"No, that was later, after Hotchkins fried my brain. My family kept threatening to put me back in the hospital and I was terrified. I'd watched Hotchkins turn perfectly intelligent people into babbling idiots. If they sent me back, he'd fry what was left of my brain cells."

"Your parents were frightened too. They didn't want to lose you."

"I know, but the shrink that I was seeing at the time told them to leave me alone. Told them I was not suicidal, just 'too intelligent for my own good.' He told them that I didn't belong in a hospital, that they should stop talking about putting me back in. I just wanted them to shut up. To leave me alone. I wanted people to stop telling me I would never hold a job, that I was sick, and might always be that way."

"Things just get started," Dr. Maynard sighed. "Like wars. People start killing each other, and soon they can't stop. No one really knows, or cares, why after a while. But your mother still wants me to give you some tests. She still thinks you have brain damage. Do you want to stay at Clarion for a couple more weeks?"

"My mother has brain damage!"

"How about San Francisco? You've been there."

No, I explained, I had already chased too many shadows there. In Mission Street pawnshops where I sold everything I owned to keep from starving. In North Beach coffeehouses and pubs where all the waiters knew Picasso, the waitresses partied with Albert Camus, and even the dish washers went shark fishing with Papa Hemingway off the coast of Cuba. I'd chased shadows in skid row dives, pigs feet floating in autopsy brine, bartenders packing revolvers and Ezra Pound look-alikes falling out by the dozen. In Ferlinghetti's City Lights bookstore, young beats clinging to the shelves like sleeping bats. On a rancid mattress in a pay-by-the-week pad, giant water bugs floating in the bathtub and a wad of eviction notices stapled to the door.

I'd studied my texts and said my mantras, waiting for Nirvana to rise out of a gallon of rosé, or Jack and his entourage to show up but they never did. Broke, and very hungry, I walked into a bookstore

146

to sell my last art history book. "Kerouac," said the store's owner, stroking his billygoat beard and showing off his bulletproof eyes, "done split to Venice, man. Best go back to the cornbelt, man. Give you five for the book, man." "Go fuck yourself . . . man," I said, tucking the book under my arm and slamming out the door, squatting that night in the bushes in Golden Gate Park, a racoon feasting on half-eaten chunks of chicken, not the first or the last time I would eat garbage to stay alive.

"New York," I guess.

"New York? That's great," Dr. Maynard said. "You're really ready for adventure, aren't you."

"Why not? I've got a friend there. His name is Flemington. I met him when I was a freshman in college."

Dr. Maynard and I shook hands and then, without warning, he reached out and hugged me, something no man had ever done.

"Goodbye," he said. "And God bless you. Drop me a line if you get the chance."

"Thank you," I said. "I'll try to do that."

CHAPTER 9

War

W*e wrapped our father's bullet belts around our scrawny waists,
stuffed newspaper into their steel helmets, and posed before the mirror in their medal-studded field jackets. Then we attacked the enemy,
screaming our hatred as we fought hand-to-hand, killing them without mercy. Our fathers' rites of passage had been war; it would also
be ours. We were anxious to become real men.*

Two military policemen at parade rest in front of St. Al-
ban's Military Hospital in Queens, sunlight flecking off their
spit-shined boots, .45 caliber revolvers clinging to their hips.
Their jaws are locked, their eyes vacantly furious. I shuffle
forward, humming, scratching my head, but they appear not
to see me.

Should I salute, the way we were taught to do in ROTC:

"Cadet Wilcox reporting for duty, sir. Cadet Wilcox re-
quests permission to enter the Captain's office, sir."

A couple more steps toward the hospital.

"YOU THERE, HALT! State your name and business."

"I'm here to see my cousin, Sergeant Douglas Boulter."

"Boulter?" the MP repeats.

"That's right, Sergeant Douglas Boulter."

"Ward?"

"I don't know," I reply, removing a wrinkled sheet of paper

from my pocket. "I just got this telegram last night telling me that he's here, that he . . ."

"Hold right here."

The second MP turns toward me, right hand resting on his .45. His eyes are whirlpools, holes, volcanos. His jaw quivers. He appears to be in a trance. I move cautiously forward, standing less than a foot from his unblinking, unyielding face. Two men. Two American males. One in uniform. One wearing a pair of cheap slacks, white shirt, the flower-patterned tie Siobhan hand-stitched for him. I stare into the MP's eyes, hating what we're doing, yet unwilling to look away. The whirlpools bubble. The volcanos explode. The voice of reason urges me to look away. I study his eyes, his hands, his feet. He studies me. The second MP returns holding a clipboard.

"You may enter," he says. "Sign here. Name. Name of patient. Purpose."

I return the clipboard.

"Enter there," says the second MP, pointing with the clipboard. "Take the elevator to the third floor. Turn right. Sign out when you leave."

The MPs return to parade rest.

A crude sign scrawled in crayon on a piece of cardboard reads:

If the patient has a fit, depress tongue, tie hands, ring.

Two rows of metal beds separated by a narrow aisle. A young man in a pair of rumpled light blue pajamas is talking excitedly into his cupped hands. He holds one hand up to his right ear, listens, laughs, nods his head. A black soldier, wrists lashed to the bedframe with rags, appears to be sleeping, or dead. The floor is is littered with trash . . . No nurses, doctors, or aides. Sergeant Boulter lies in the fourth bed down.

"Doug," I whisper. "Doug, it's me, your cousin."

He opens his eyes, bewildered, smiling.

"Is that you? Really you? Damn, it's been a long time. A long time. Why just look at you, boy. You're looking good, real good. Sharp, real sharp. You're lookin' strack."

In bed four, a young man attempts to break free from the

canvas straps that lash him to the bedframe. He is shouting, and threatening to kill me. When he struggles, the row of medals pinned to his bedspread bob up and down like tiny marionettes. Doug waves toward the boy.

"Take it easy, Sarge. This isn't a gook. It's my cousin, from Iowa. My own kin, Johnnie." The patient struggles and shouts. Doug motions me closer, whispers.

"Just don't pay that jarhead any mind. He doesn't mean it. It's a damn shame. Boy's entire platoon got wiped out. Most new in-country and he's the CO. Found that poor boy wandering around stark naked. Say he killed three VC with his bare hands. Kid's gone, that's all there is to it. Brought back his body, left his mind over there in the Nam."

Doug catches me staring at his black and blue arms.

"Yeah, the doctors don't know what's wrong with me, so they keep blowing air into my brain. Think I've got a collapsed blood vessel maybe. It hurts. Oh man, does it hurt when they do those tests. Sometimes I think I'm gonna go insane when they're blowing air up there. I mean time just stands still. Dead still, like days, weeks, are passing. Bad news, bad, bad news. I'd like to go home, but they won't let me."

Bed six is raving. Doug props himself up on his elbows, and I sit on his bed so our faces are nearly touching.

"Oh, that boy," he says. "Twenty-two. Looks fifty, don't he? College boy, I guess. Brownbar straight out of ROTC. Put him right into the shit and he couldn't hack it. Position got overrun by the NVA the first week he was there and he cracked. Took off. Brought him in here just a few days ago. Shoot him full of morphine. Shuts him up for a while. Be an addict if he ever does go home. Oh man, it's pitiful. See that one down there, third bed up from the end on the other side. Somthin's eatin' up his insides. Weighs about 90 pounds. Gonna let him go home this weekend to see his kin, then he'll probably just come back in here and die."

Bed by bed, Doug tells me the soldiers' stories, occasionally closing his eyes to rest. He asks about about my folks and I answer that they're just fine. We reminisce for a while, laughing about the time my father took us fishing and we caught a boatload of bluegills, gutting and dipping them in eggs and bread crumbs then cooking them over our campfire. The moon was full and we toasted marshmallows and told ghost stories, falling asleep to the soft crackling of our fire and the wind in the trees.

"Boy," Doug sighs. "We sure were dirt poor, weren't we? I remember your folks bringin' food over so we didn't starve clear to death, and hell, they didn't have a pot to piss in themselves. Got good hearts, your folks. Times were tough when we were kids. Military just seemed like the best way to go for me. One way to get a clean bed and three squares a day. No regrets. None. Been a good life. Fed my family. Kept a roof over my kids' heads. Can't complain."

Doug shows me some snapshots of his wife and kids, two grinning little boys, a girl with her front teeth missing, standing outside an Air Force barracks. He puts the photos away and closes his eyes.

"Well," I say, resting my hand on his arm, "I guess I'd better be going so you can get some rest."

"Yeah," he sighs. "I hate to admit it, but I do feel kinda worn out. But listen, you come back to see me, hear? I don't know how long I'll be in here, but you come on back. We'll tell some more stories. Gosh, I'd like to see your mom and dad again. I miss them. I'll bet you do, too."

"Yeah," I say. "I miss them."

I stand to leave, but Doug waves me back to the bed.

"One more thing," he says, motioning about the room. "I just don't go for this thing. Almost twenty years in the military, but not this. Just don't you go over there to Vietnam, you hear?"

I stood by Doug's bed, wishing I could tell him about the night I watched a razor open ugly canyons in my forearms, blood pouring into the sink while I waited for an angel to land on the back of my hand or darkness to buckle my knees. But nothing happened. I pulled the stopper closed, curious to see how long it would take the sink to fill, surprised at the speed with which red and white corpuscles turn to Jell-o, watching my life run down the drain, feeling little more than boredom.

A few weeks after that, I reported to the induction center at Fort Des Moines, stripped naked as ordered, stood naked as ordered, tried to urinate into the little bottle I'd been given, as ordered. We stood in lines in front of the piss troughs, shaking and waving our manhood over our bottles while a sergeant walked behind us with a long thin rod, threatening to insert it into our uretha if we didn't hurry up and follow orders. "Piss in those bottles boys," he shouted. "We don't have all day. If you don't want to give it to us, we'll just have to take it from you. Come on, boys, squeeze it out. PISS, boys, PISS." A couple of WACs walked the line, pointing at young draftees. "Oh," said one, "look at that thing. Couldn't even please a mouse with that, let alone a woman." "Woopadoop," her partner replied. "Looks like that one done shrunk in the laundry."

We sat naked all morning on metal chairs while army doctors tested our eyesight and hearing. We walked naked from table to table, filling out forms and answering questions about our health, and whether or not we were members of "subversive" organizations like the National Association for the Advancement of Colored People, the Socialist Discussion Club, and Fair Play For Cuba. I checked all of the above and a sergeant took me into another room, demanding to know who forced me to attend subversive meetings, and who made me join communist organizations.

"There must be communists on your campus," he said.

"I've never met one," I replied.

"Then who makes you attend them meetings?"

"No one," I said. "I support Fidel Castro because he overthrew Batista. I joined the Socialist Discussion Club because it looked like an interesting group, and I believe in what the NAACP's doing to help colored people, that's all. Mostly, I'm just curious, Sergeant."

I thought he might hit me, but he just turned and walked away. We were asked to check childhood illnesses or diseases and again I answered truthfully, checking whooping cough, pneumonia, bronchitis, allergies, hay fever, and sinus problems.

"Jesus Christ, Hamlet," another sergeant screamed, scanning my sheet. "Have you ever had a baby?"

"No, sir," I quipped, "but I'm working on it."

Recruits behind me laughed. I smiled.

"Don't call me sir," he screamed. "And knock that shit eatin' grin off your face before I knock it off for you."

"Yes, sir," I said.

At noon, we were told to put on our clothes and were taken downstairs to a lunch of T-bone steak, baked potatoes, and salad, after which we returned to the induction area, where we again stripped naked. One form asked whether we had "homosexual tendencies" and I checked "yes." I sat on a metal chair, naked, a cloth bag containing my car keys and wallet in my hand. The uniformed psychologist stared for a long time at my form, then at me, then back to the form. Suddenly he screamed:

"HOW LONG HAVE YOU BEEN ACTIVE?"

"What?" I replied. "Active in what?"

"HOW LONG HAVE YOU BEEN SUCKING COCKS?"

"I am not a homosexual," I said.

"Yes you are. You said so, right here on this form. Right here. You checked it."

I looked around the room. Naked recruits were blushing, their bodies turning various shades of shame. I gripped the metal chair until my hands went numb, resisting the urge to smash it over my interrogator's head. No, I didn't want to be in his fucking army. Like the psychiatric hospitals I'd been in, it was obvious that the military was run by sadomasochistic assholes. I'd already had my head shaved, already been forced to wear a prison uniform, already been put through too many degrading ceremonies. If they wanted me in their big badass army, they would have to hear what I had to say.

It was 1960. America was not at war. Had it been, I might have accepted their invitation to join up. I wasn't afraid of dying, and still liked violence, though I didn't like to admit it. I just couldn't stand boredom and stupidity. Seventy-two hours in the army and they would have me locked up in the brig. Five minutes in the brig and I would swing on one of the guards. Induction into the military would mean a life sentence in Fort Leavenworth. I couldn't quite understand how that would benefit me, or my country.

"No, sir," I replied, politely but firmly. "I am not a homosexual."

"Do you suck cocks?"

"No sir, I never have."

"Do you like it up the ass?"

"No, I've never done that."

"Listen, you say you're a queer. Either you are, or you're not. We don't want queers in this man's army."

"I never said I was 'queer.' I said I have 'homosexual tendencies.' Everyone does. Look at Julius Caesar. Wasn't he a great soldier? And the Roman Legions, weren't they brave? Didn't they win a lot of battles?"

"But you checked it. Right here. Look."

"I checked that little box, but what I meant is sometimes I look at a man and find him attractive. For example, Michelangelo's statue, 'David.' Isn't he beautiful? Don't you find Greek figures, the ones of naked athletes, sensuous? Most men do. They just don't want to admit it, that's all."

"Hell no, that's not what men do. That's what queers do. NOT men."

"I'm not a homosexual. Never have been. I like having sex with women. I just wanted to answer honestly, that's all. You asked me a question, and I gave you an answer."

"I'll ask you again," he shouted, even louder this time. "HOW LONG HAVE YOU BEEN ACTIVE?"

"And I'll tell you again. Everyone has 'homosexual tendencies.' Even you. Men look at men and find them attractive. Women look at women and find them attractive. People look at people and find them attractive. So what? Who cares? That doesn't mean everyone wants to have sex with everyone else on earth."

"Well, I'm gonna put down here that you're queer."

"You can put down anything you want, but that's not what I said, and that's not what I meant."

The psychologist looked at the scars on my arms.

"Tried to kill yourself?"

"No."

"What are those?"

"Scars."

"I can see that. You slit your wrists. Why'd you want to die?"

"I didn't."

"People don't slit their wrists unless they want to die."

"Oh yes, they do it all the time. In every hospital I was ever in I saw women who'd cut their wrists, but I never met one who really wanted to die. They just wanted to get away from a bad situation, like husbands who were beating them up, bad marriages, things like that. Didn't think there was any other way out."

"What are you talking about?"

"I said I didn't want to die. Ask Dr. Rice. He's a psychiatrist. He'll tell you."

"But you're not a woman."

"True, but I just wanted to escape."

"Escape what?"

"Being told I was crazy. Being told by psychiatirsts that I would never be able to hold a job, that I would have nervous breakdowns all my life, that I would become psychotic by the age of thirty-five, that my father hated me, that I belonged in nuthouses, that I would always be some kind of psychic invalid, that I had brain damage, that I should grow up, be a man, settle down, become a hole, live a life of quiet desperation, kill the muse, kill myself but slowly and surely, the way everyone else does."

"Well, I don't know if you were crazy or not, but slitting your wrists is pretty damn sick if you ask me. And I don't really care if you're queer or not. But this is gonna look real bad on your record, son. Follow you around for the rest of your life. You'll never be able to get a good job. Never run for public office. Never do anything really important unless you've been in the service. Never be the President."

"The President of what?" I laughed.

"The United States," he said.

"I don't think they let ex-mental patients do that."

"Do what?"

"Be the President," I replied, laughing even harder. He stared at me and wrote something in his little book. Apparently, he didn't get the joke.

Years before, in ROTC, shoes spit-shined, eagle pinned exactly a quarter inch from this or that button, head shaved, I had marched round and round the fieldhouse with hundreds of young student cadets. The cadet commander looked and talked like Peter Lorre and everyone said he was "one of those." He shouted orders over a loudspeaker while we stumbled and slammed into one another, lurching forward and back, trying to move in smooth formation but bumping about like drunken horses, rather than real soldiers. I enjoyed wearing my uniform. It was comfortable and very warm in winter. Cocking my officer's hat to one side, I felt dashing, even rather heroic as I passed young women walking to and from class. But no matter how hard I tried to keep the eagles straight on my lapels, they would always slip sideways. I forgot, or couldn't afford, to cut my hair once a week. I washed dishes in the dormitory from 5:00 a.m. to 8:00 a.m. every morning, and when I arrived at drill my spit-shined shoes were often stained with syrup and eggs. "Cadet Wilcox," the lieutenant screamed, "I'm giving you two demerits. I wanna see my own pretty face in them shoes of yours. I wanna see that hair cut so you don't look like some creepy crawlin' beatnik type. I wanna see your eagles standin' up straight and stiff just like your little dick does in the morning."

One afternoon, we were taking a multiple choice exam. Something about a U.S. Air Force weapons system. Concentric rings of destruction. The amount of firepower a particular airplane could deliver. Abstract and, it occurred to me, very stupid questions. I saw rabbits lying on their sides in the snow, blood soaking out of their mouths, their hind legs twitching and kicking. Soldiers die that way, said my father. Like rabbits, bleeding, kicking. I put my boot on the rabbit's head, giving a quick decapitating yank on its hind legs. Like soldiers, kicking and defecating in the snow. I stared at the test sheet. We were talking about bombing human beings, not lamp posts or dandelions or rabbits. I wrote "none of the above" in the margin. I hadn't gone rabbit hunting for years, and didn't want to start hunting humans now. I wanted to be a poet, not a soldier.

The train lurches into Manhattan, rocking so hard that I think it's going to leave the tracks. Across from me a man is scanning the *Daily News*. **"Light at the end of the tunnel,"** announces one headline. The train slams to a stop. People zombie off, on. I close my eyes, trying to squeeze out the

MPs' eyes, the screams, the hollow terror in bed five's eyes, the way bed four snapped his teeth at me, the little puppets that danced, mockingly, when he struggled and wept. One week later another telegram arrives at Siobhan's apartment. Sergeant Boulter, it says, is dead.

"But you've got to give it back," Siobhan is screaming into the receiver, huge tears rolling down her cheeks. "You promised. You said if I cleaned the place up you'd give it back. It's mine. You owe it to me. I want it back."

I set my beer can on the window ledge and snatch the phone out of her hand.

"Listen," I shout into the receiver, "this is Thomas P. O' Grady, Attorney at Law. Yes, that's right, we've spoken before. You give this poor woman back her deposit or I'm gonna file a lawsuit against you, I'm gonna come down there with some goons from the South Village and break your kneecaps, I'm gonna hire a hitman to knock a home-run with your head, I'm gonna pay one of my junkie friends to give you flying lessons, I'm gonna get one of the pyromaniacs on the block to. . . .

"I'm gonna kill you, and all your scumbag slumlord friends," I shout, ripping the dead phone from the wall and tossing it across the room. Whenever I called to ask Siobhan's landlord to turn the heat back on or make repairs he just laughed at me. Not at my amateur acting—I would always pose as a lawyer—but at the idea that he, a slumlord, could be held accountable for anything. After all, the lease clearly states that the building's owner, not his tenants, holds all of the power. 605 East Sixth Street is his *private* property and if he feels like turning off the heat in January, he will. If he wishes to allow rats to live in *his* hallways, he will. If he doesn't feel like providing garbage cans, he won't. If he doesn't care to make repairs, so what? If he feels like throwing a family into the streets, he will.

We carry Siobhan's things downstairs, loading them into a borrowed car. Puppy sits in the driver's seat, smiling and drooling on the wheel. Teresa holds Windsong, cooing into her ear and stroking her hair. Windsong laughs and pinches Teresa's nose and Teresa makes her huge brown eyes swell, comically rolling them back and forth. Windsong giggles and holds Teresa around the neck. Teresa is wearing a short, very faded green dress. Her knees are badly bruised and she has a black eye. Her bare feet are too small, even for her stunted body. She claims she's thirteen, Siobhan and I think she might be ten.

"We're gonna move too, you know that?" Teresa says.

"No, where?" Siobhan replies.

"Back to Puerto Rico, man. My dad's built a really big house there. Huge fucking place. Really big, man. Twelve bathrooms. Yeah, we're gonna move. Next week."

In warm weather, Teresa would descend the fire escape, sitting outside Siobhan's window and catwatching the people inside. Sometimes she simply jumped, without invitation, into the apartment, balancing on her hands and walking back and forth across the floor to amuse Windsong. If we ignored her she would stand on her head for five minutes, wagging her double jointed tongue and wiggling her long pointy ears. Teresa liked to sit beside Windsong's basket, singing lullabies in Spanish and making up stories about little girls whose fathers rode great white horses across the sky. Teresa rode Windsong around the apartment on her back, prancing and winnowing and bucking. Sometimes she stayed for a few minutes. When she was smoking pot she stayed for hours.

"Oh yeah, man," she would say. "My dad owns three airplanes. And sometimes he takes me for rides in them. We fly to Puerto Rico to see my grandmother. I get to do it myself, man. Fly a plane. You ever do that, man?"

"No, Teresa."

"I have. It's easy, man. It's fun. You just take the wheel like this, ZOOOM ZOOOM. It's simple. My dad showed me how to do it. No problem. I fly him around, you now. We get to go a lot of places together."

"Where do you live now?" Siobhan asked.

"Oh, we live in a really huge house, way uptown. You don't know my neighborhood. It's not like this. It's nice. No dogshit on the sidewalks. No fucking landlords. No junkies, man. They don't allow them up there. Not where my dad lives. Cause everybody up there's got their own house, and they just kick the junkies' asses outa there. We live there. Just him and me."

"Where's your mother?"

"I don't got no mother."

"Sisters, brothers?"

"No, they all died."

"Died?"

"Yeah. They didn't like me, so they died."

"Why didn't they like you?"

"I don't know."

"Oh, so they died."

"That's what I'm tellin you."

"How'd your father get so much money?"

"He just makes it, that's all."

"How?"

"I don't know. I seen him do it. One time, he made a million dollars. That's the truth, man. I saw it with my own eyes."

Siobhan throws garbage bags stuffed with her treasures into the trunk.

"You really movin' out of the neighborhood?" Teresa asks again, kissing Windsong on the cheek.

"Yes," Siobhan answers, "but you can come visit us."

"Where you goin', Puerto Rico?"

"No, out to the country."

"What country?"

"Just, well, out to Pennsylvania, Teresa."

"Oh yeah, man. My dad owns Pennsylvania. I fly there all the time. I been there lotsa times."

In the spring of 1967, Siobhan moved into a tiny house in New Jersey and I tried to live there for a while, driving to Trenton every morning in a beat-up, $49.50 Plymouth. The house had a tiny bathroom, but no hot water or shower, so I rose every morning at five, heating pots of water on the stove and taking sponge baths, ironing one of my two shirts and a pair of slacks, knotting my flowerpatch tie and heading off to the commuter train. I had secured a temporary job with the Office of Economic Opportunity, the coordinating agency for President Johnson's so-called War on Poverty. I sat at my desk, typing memos and writing poetry on the backs of envelopes.

"You should take advantage of this thing before it ends," said Dr. Penny, the woman who interviewed me. "There's money to be made. Jobs are rampant, and lucrative."

I opened Dr. Penny's mail every day, stacking her dividends from oil companies in one pile, her government paychecks from the three anti-poverty programs she directed in another. I ran down to the corner deli to fetch Penny white turkey sandwiches on white bread with Russian dressing, drove out to the Bronx to fix her speeding tickets, and acted as her secretary.

"Hello," a very important, urgent voice, would say. "This is Dr. Snorkal's secretary calling for Dr. Snorkal who wishes to speak with Dr. Penny. Is Dr. Penny in?"

"Who?" I would answer, trying to humiliate the secretary.

"DOCTOR SNORKAL," the voice replied, *Chair of the task force on poverty, industrialism, development, early childhood disorders, and building better schools.*"

"Oh yes," I would sigh. "Well, Dr. Penny is in a *very* important meeting, but perhaps I could have her get back to Dr. Snorkal this afternoon."

Penny's policy was quite simple: She refused to speak to anyone right away, unless they were phoning from the White House. Mornings, I scribbled messages on little squares of paper, throwing the less important callers in the wastebasket, returning "urgent" calls in the afternoon.

"This is Dr. Wilcox calling for Dr. Penny's office," I said, lowering my voice to a pompous baritone, with an ever so slight British inflection. "Is Dr. Snorkal in? This is quite urgent. Dr. Penny is leaving town for the next decade and she must speak to Dr. Snorkal at once."

"I'm sorry, Dr. Wilcox," the voice repaying my earlier rebuff, "but Dr. Snorkal is in a very important meeting right now, and can not be reached. If Dr. Penny wishes to leave a message, perhaps Dr. Snorkal could get back to her in the near future."

"Listen, you called this morning, wishing to speak to Dr. Penny, *Executive Director of Children's Programs, the Task Force On the Elderly, Afterschool Programs, Before School Programs, the*

Committee to Purge Violence From Our Schools, the Committee to Reform Education, The Agency to Improve Cognitive Development in the Homeless. She is available NOW, just now . . . for only a . . . few . . . moments . . . Does Dr. Snorkal wish to speak to her or not? I don't have time to waste."

"Well, of course he does," replied the voice, deeply impressed by my abrasive condescension. "He does, but he's in a meeting with the Chairman of the *Commission on Building Neighborhood Networking in Disadvantaged and Culturally Deprived Neighborhoods Amidst the Blight of Poverty, Disease, and Deteriorating Socio-Economic Development in our Ghettos.*"

"Fine," I hissed. "Dr. Snorkal's expertise is well known and respected. He's making a real contribution to the war on poverty. But you must understand," I whispered into the receiver, "this is a crisis . . ." I drew out the words, turning two syllables into six. 'Cr..i..s..i..s..sisssss,' I hissed, enjoying the way this word sounded, pausing, jotting a line or two of poetry on the back of a sheet of anti-poverty stationery.

"Dr. Penny is here, RIGHT NOW, on the other line, WAITING . . ."

"O.K., I'll see if I can reach Dr. Snorkal. Please hold."

"Yes, this is Dr. Snorkal speaking," the voice breathless, irritated. "I just left the meeting of the *Chairs on Chairing the Next Symposium on Chairs,* but I'm afraid I have only a few minutes. We are in rather a serious crisis here."

"Milton? Is that you?" Penny sang, "I've been trying to get ahold of you for days."

"Oh, Penny," Milton moaned, "my dear Pen, how very good of you to call. Yes, the funding did come through. Yes, it's very exciting. We're planning a colloquium in May. Yes, I'll be meeting with Sergeant Shriver this week. Yes, Dr. K. will meet you at the Copley Plaza on Friday. Great steamed clams there. Yes, I will be able to speak at the symposium in June. Yes, the fee is quite acceptable. Yes . . ."

Young black men in white shirts and alligator skin shoes pushed brooms around the office, preparing, I was told, to enter the job market after a year or two with "The Job Corps." When I asked Penny how much they made—more than I did I hoped—she looked at me as though I asked what color underwear she was wearing.

161

"But I don't understand," I told Dr. Penny's administrative assistant. "Penny makes sixty thousand dollars a year. The switchboard operator makes six. I'm making minimum wage."

"Wages aren't the point right now," she answered.

"Money's not the point?"

"Not really. The point is to get to the root of the problem."

"But the root *is* money. Some people have too much. Some people don't have any."

"No, no, no," she said, reaching into her desk for a handful of cookies. "That's just nonsense, kneejerk Marxism. Money is only a symptom. Once we understand the symptoms well enough, we'll come up with the cure. It just takes time. Penny is an expert. You can learn a lot from her if you're just willing to listen."

I responded to letters from people inviting Dr. Penny to attend important, sometimes urgent, seminars and colloquia, explaining that she must be paid a substantial fee, that the fee must be received in advance, and that all accommodations, airfare, meals, and gratuities must be paid by the invitee. Right now, I wrote, we are in a crisis. President Johnson has said that he wants to end poverty. Dr. Penny is in great demand. I have no time to negotiate. Take it or leave it.

One morning, Dr. B. Bilston, Director of *Children Tutoring Children Who Need Tutoring in Tutoring,* (a program to develop motor coordination, improve cognitive skills, and raise test scores in disadvantaged youth,) stood a short distance from my desk, monologuing about her discovery that poor children do less well than their "advantaged" peers on cognitive skills tests. Maria, a ten-year-old Puerto Rican girl who liked to watch me type, was telling me a story. "Well," she said, "so that fat motherfucker wanted my pen and I wouldn't give it to her, so she calls me a whore and I slap her fucking face, and . . ."

"Maria," Dr. Bilston interrupted, "isn't there some other way to describe your friend?"

"She ain't my friend," Maria said.

"But some other language. Might we not express ourselves in some other, more meaningful way?"

"But," Marie said, her brown eyes glowing with conviction, "but she *is* a fat motherfucker. What can I say, man?"

I stopped typing, laughing until tears ran down my cheeks, unable to stop even when Dr. Bilston gave me a most admonishing wave of her hand. I laughed and cried. Maria started another story. Dr. Bilston walked away.

I was invited to seminars or colloquia, and as long as I listened quietly Penny didn't mind. She considered me rather harmless, and tolerated my pleasant crankiness. Only when I talked about my own experiences did she get upset. Sometimes, it was difficult to keep quiet. From the commuter train's window I could see smoke billowing out of Newark. Commuters held their newspapers in front of their faces like shields. The riots were spreading across America, the war on poverty was not.

On weekends I took Windsong for outings along the Delaware River, watching her chase after the ducks, quacking and waving her arms, standing quite still with surprise when they flew away. We threw crusts of bread into the canal and I held her in my lap and we laughed at the ducks' silly scramble. We walked over to New Hope, picnicking beside the canal that runs through the village. Mules plodded along the towpath, pulling barges filled with tourists who waved to us passing by. After lunch we lay on our backs, basking in the sun and singing. Puppy would breaststroke back and forth across the canal, snapping at the water with his great canine teeth, his one great maniacal eye scanning for things to kill. Later, Windsong sat next to me on a barstool, sipping birch beer while I exchanged stories with my favorite bartender, and drank myself into a very pleasant stupor.

On the way to Trenton one morning the Plymouth blew up, billowing black smoke, refusing to budge. Commuters raced by on their way to the train. I missed work that day, arrived late the next, and the next. I returned from the city around seven or eight, most always drunk from riding in the club car from New York to Trenton, sometimes falling asleep and riding on to Philadelphia, where the conductor shook me awake and guided me to the other side of the tracks. Out of bed again at 4:30, riding the train, the subway, walking, arriving late to work, swilling coffee all day to stay awake.

Siobhan wasn't surprised when I told her I was going back to the Lower East Side. I just could not control my nerves. A bird rustling in the bushes made me jump, legs set wide apart, hands raised, ready to kill. The quiet terrified me, and I suffered from insomnia. Watching people paint their houses, pick up sticks and mow their yards filled me with dread. I was disoriented and frightened in the country.

Siobhan's neighbors went to church, belonged to Kiwanis, the American Legion, Rotary, Knights of Columbus. They paid taxes, voted in elections, enrolled their kids in Little League and Boy Scouts, had checking and savings accounts, burial plots, life insurance, retirement plans. They watched t.v., took their elderly parents out to lunch on Sundays, twisted their children's socks into neat little balls, put things away in mothball closets, wrapped the Christmas tree decorations carefully each year and stored them in the garage.

I didn't dislike them. That wasn't the problem at all. It was just that I was backing up with dread. My heart wouldn't drain. I couldn't control the fear. It lodged in my chest, bending me double with its weight. It floated through my veins like an air bubble, riding toward disaster. I couldn't keep it down. The trap was being set. One leg already inside. Soon, I would be forced to gnaw myself loose. Stay and become a hole, unwilling to climb out of myself; unable to see the bottom.

CHAPTER 10

The Last Party

John moved out of his pad on East 7th, found a loft on East Broadway, and set up a cot for me in the middle of his huge shadowy space. Unlike my hippie beatnik junkie friends, he had always been responsible, but now he quit his uptown job and was freelance editing. I found a job indexing books, and kept working day and night without sleep until one afternoon I was lying on my cot, struggling to come down from a week-long amphetamine rush. A giant white bird fluttered out of the ceiling, perched on my chest, and stared into my eyes. The bird had great ugly feet and it was very heavy and it just squatted there, looking into me. I couldn't breathe, but the bird wouldn't lift its feet or flap its wings and it didn't seem to have anything profound or metaphysical to say and I finally passed out from fear, or boredom.

John and I were falling behind in the rent, eating less, drinking more, and didn't have much left to lose, so we decided to have a party. We invited everyone we knew on the Lower East Side to a costume party and they invited everyone they knew and by 11:00 a.m. the crowd was ass to elbow and everyone brought lots to drink or smoke so that we were dancing sweating and jiving drunk drugged to the Supremes Four Tops Temptations Beatles shoving thigh-to-thigh grinning and hip fucking each other. The police arrived in their own costumes, complaining about the noise and trying to shake us down for a bit of change. John was wearing a giant papier maché codspiece (he was supposed to be Bacchus), and he stood in the doorway, the codspiece wobbling back and forth, telling the cops to come in and join the fun, but they just shrugged, gave him their best "we'll kick your ass later" smiles, and left.

Then Beryl stepped inside. She was wearing a silky green dress and high-heeled red shoes and she stood there, as she often did, waiting for the lights to come up, knowing the audience was trying to catch its breath because Beryl was Marilyn Monroe and Bridget Bardot and Eva Marie Saint, all in one human form, one costume, and my own lights came up hard and fast. I took her hand, placing it on my light, and she laughed and we danced but the crowd was sucking up alcohol fast so I wandered about, collecting wads of money for the next booze run, talking to people I knew and didn't know, making passes at women, turning down offers from men. I tried to cheer up Don and Jerry, dressed as identical twin grim reapers, because their pet blue jay had passed away, telling them I was terribly sorry to hear about their loss, that I loved that bird as though it were my own child, and that I would miss it always. Don started to cry. He was very fond of Broadway musicals and the bird could whistle tunes from "The King and I" and many other shows, and one day it caught a wicked cold. Don and Jerry gave it lots of vitamin C and antibiotics and even took it to their own physician, demanding that he find some ornithology intensive care unit for their pet, praying for a miracle cure, holding a healing seance, but the two lovers found their bird one morning, still wrapped in the little velvet gown that one of their friends had designed for it, lying on its back, legs up, dead inside the grand cottage—miniature antiques, a courtyard with a tiny marble bath, and a master bedroom in which the bird could lie in bed looking at itself in wall-to-wall mirrors—Don and Jerry had lovingly crafted for their singer.

John had been performing in an off-Broadway play, written by a friend of his. The band from the play were all tough street boys from Brooklyn and I didn't like them because they acted like such hardasses and I thought I was a bigger hardass. John insisted on inviting them to the party, and after wandering around for about an hour, puffing here and slurping there, it occurred to my dim-lit brain that I hadn't seen Beryl for a very long time, so I walked out to the landing, looked up the stairs leading to the roof, heard some very familiar noises and started to climb. The band's drummer, disguised as Ringo Starr, had his pants unzipped but not down, he was too street smart for that, and was rolling in and out of Beryl, who had her dress hiked up and her own pink panties around her ankles, and when I charged up the stairs Ringo kicked me, Dylan Thomas, in the chest and I rolled back to the bottom gasping and cursing Ringo, who was stumbling over my face on his way to the street, and I hit the door just as Beryl Bardot came down the stairs without her shoes, because I had them in my hand, but before I could slam the door in her face she spread-eagled in the frame screaming that she wanted her shoes she wanted to come back to the party she wanted her bottle of Chivas Regal back and I was pushing her out and John was helping me and she was kicking and throwing punches and someone tossed one of her shoes into the hallway and she took the bait, reaching for it, and I knocked the door shut, flowing back into the humping crowd of witches and warlocks and clowns and Rolling Stone look-alikes and even a young girl dressed, she thought, like a tree or maybe she was a flower and everyone was cheering because the booze runners had arrived with enough alcohol to keep us going for days.

I woke tangled in costumes and bodies, heads and chests and legs, recalling dimly that the body I was closest too had said, just as the sun peaked into the loft, "I thought you'd never ask," and when we made love under a table I liked her very much. But I knew that John would soon be married, that this was our last party, that people were starting to disappear, and a few days later John and I mixed a thermos of orange juice and vodka, locked the door to the loft and took the train to Queens, sipping our libation, the two of us in borrowed suits. The guests drank champagne before the wedding and when John and his bride said "I do" a band struck up "Yesterday" and I danced with one of the bride's cousins, who was drunk enough to tell me that her former husband called her "M.C." "M.C.?" I asked, rubbing my tongue in and out of her ear as we danced. "Yes," she giggled. "Multi-Come."

Later, I sat in the kitchen with the black caterers, drinking and telling stories, and John's bride drove her husband and me into Manhattan, me lying in the back seat dreaming of "M.C." Margo stopped on West Fourth and I stumbled from the car, confused and hurt and having no idea where I would spend the night because I had merely assumed that the three of us would live happily together in John's loft, scraping by on office temps and visits to pawn shops, as John and I and our friends had done always, but watching the taillights swirl away in the night I realized that once again I was homeless, and I found a hotel by the week, took off my borrowed suit, counted out my money, made sure I still had M.C.'s address and phone number on the back of a gum wrapper, and fell alseep thinking about the great party John and I had thrown for all of our old friends and lovers, and wondering where I would live after the week at the hotel ran out, and when I might see Beryl again, and whether she might have a place and how I might convince her to let me stay there.

CHAPTER 11

Beginnings and Endings

S*oldiers firing volleys over the dead, the drift of taps and tears, the sounds of our nation at war. I stood next to my mother, unwilling to look into her eyes because I did not have forgiveness in my heart; because I did not wish to break her heart. She wept but I could not embrace her, not even to honor Sergeant Boulter. The rows of white tombstones rising and falling toward the horizon, tipped here and there with the little black boats of open graves, eviscerating taps, the honor guard's volleys like firing squads.*

I had been living in a basement room on Mott Street, paying my weekly rent to an old demon who smoked Turkish cigarettes and blew his nose on the sleeves of his terrycloth bathrobe. His pudgy toes protruded from holes in his moth-eaten sheepskin slippers, and his tiny swamp eyes trickled down his cheeks when he talked about the good old days in Palermo. When I was late with the rent or complained about water dripping on my bed or the clogged toilet or the herds of black bugs that roamed the walls of my room—the street lights magnifying them into Buffalo shadows—he would sniffle, blow his nose on his sleeve, and roll his eyes toward the statue of the Virgin Mary hanging on a nail next to a map of his beloved Sicily.

"I dunna know nothin'," he would sigh. "'cept who owns a

this a building. Me, I only work for a livn'. All a my life. Work for a livin'. They a nice boys. Real a nice. Like a to keep things a nice, know a what I meana? Noa trouble, that's all. You be a nice to a them, they be a nice to a you, that's all. Everytings a nice. That's all. You donna be nice, well. Whata can I say? I dunno. Maybe I have a to speak to them."

In the middle of the block was a deli, and I used to go there to hear the walls talk. "Oughta that," said the ancient woman behind the counter whenever I asked for anything. "Oughta that today." "American cheese?" "Oughta that." "Salami?" "Oughta that." I walked around the store, listening to the walls. The old woman watched me. "White bread?" "Oughta that." A white Cadillac was often parked in front of the deli, and one day it made the centerfold of the *Daily News,* the driver slumped behind the wheel, blood draining from a couple of holes in his forehead. I went to the deli. "Oughta that," the old woman said when I asked for peanut butter. A black Cadillac was parked in front, and the walls of the store were still talking.

I walked to a nasty little bar on Houston Street, just across the street from a cockroach pad Beryl and I rented by the week after she returned from Washington with a pocketful of cash (I was broke and homeless again), most of which we promply drank up in Stanley's and the Old Reliable. With our last twenty dollars we rented two rooms in a building that, had it been a ship, would be sitting on the bottom of the sea. The bar was a hangout for puffy-faced punks who'd been passed over for promotion by the mob, wannabe mobsters who stood around in a cloud of stale cigar smoke, hats pulled down over their hairy ears, scratching their swollen guts and hoping that Hollywood would bit-cast them in some thriller about organized crime. I made quite a bit of money off the punks by betting on a young heavyweight fighter called Cassius Clay, later, Muhammad Ali.

"Punk," the punks at the bar would scream. "Loudmouth bum. Cuntlapper can't fight. Just with his big fat mouth, thas all. Float like a butterly sting like a bee my fucking ass. That black sonofabitch'll go down, and when he does he won't be gettin' up."

"Wanna bet," I would ask.

"Bet?"

"Yeah, put some money on the next fight?"

"Fight?"

"Yeah, you know, the one with Liston."

"Liston's gonna kill the bum no fight."

"No fight? Twenty bucks, no fight?"

"You wanna lose your money?"

"No, I wanna win, cause that's what Cassius is gonna do, knock Sonny Liston on his ass, out cold, in a couple of rounds."

"Cassius smassius, fuck him."

"Sure, but twenty?"

"Hell yes, twenty or a thousand, who the fuck cares. Man's goin' down. That'll shut his big mouth."

"Fine. Twenty it is."

Man did go down, but it wasn't my fighter. The punks never seemed to learn, and I kept making money.

One night the old wino who swept the hallways in our building fell to the butt-littered floor of the bar, clutching his chest and moaning. No one seemed to notice that he was dying, so I went into a phone booth and told the cops to bring an ambulance. The next night one of the pitbulls who'd flunked Garroting I, or could never learn to attach a silencer to the barrel of his revolver, approached me.

"You the fucking asshole who called the cops last night," he demanded, blowing Cuban smoke in my face.

"Yeah," I said, "I called an ambulance, not the cops. The guy was dying, what'd you expect me to do?"

"Well," said pitbull, looking around for the cameras, "next fucking time you fucking call the fucking cops you're the one who'll be needin' a fuckin' ambulance."

I slugged down my shot, chased it with beer and leaned forward, smiling.

"So you just wanted me to let the guy die, right? Just let him lie on the floor and fucking die."

"What's so fuckin' funny you think it's fuckin' funny to fuckin' call the fuckin' cops you don't know nothin' 'bout fuckin' callin' nobody you fuckin' little faggot."

I told this story to the former boxer who lived just below our pad. "You want me to go down there break that punk's fuckin' head?" he said. The boxer had two kids, Kitty bad and Kitty good, and when he called them he dropped the Kitty. "Bad," he would scream, "bring me my shoes." "Good, take out the garbage." "Bad, go feed the cat." "Kids," said the boxer, "are just like dogs. You got to train 'em when they're young. I toilet-trained Kitty and Bitty by wiping their noses in their own shit. They learned all right." The boxer's young wife said very little, padding about in a pair of Mickey Mouse slippers, opening cans of beer, cooking pots of Spaghetti-O's for Kitty bad and Kitty good. He talked about the fights he'd won, and almost won, the breaks he'd had, and almost had, the time he'd been asked to fix a fight but refused and things just got worse after that. I said everybody in that building must have had bad breaks or we wouldn't be there. "Fuck the people in this building," said the boxer. "They're nothin' but bums. That's why they're here." Someday he and Mary Kay were going to move out, buy a house by the ocean, maybe get a car. Mary Kay opened another beer for the boxer, and one for me. Kitty and Kitty sat on a broken-down bed behind a plastic curtain, watching a t.v. not much bigger than a loaf of bread. The boxer usually fell asleep at the table around nine o'clock.

I went to a little diner off Houston. No one was ever in the place and the old man behind the counter was always glad to see me. I ordered spaghetti with mussel sauce, and he steamed and chopped the shellfish, mixed in garlic and basil, heated a pan of tomato sauce, poured the sauce and mussels over a steaming bowl of spaghetti, and filled a milk glass with home-brewed red wine. He was a great cook and very kind to me, as people are to the dim-witted. At a back table, the cook's son and his friends counted out huge piles of money, shoving it around like a bread dough, talking and drinking wine. The old fellow kept pouring wine into my glass and ladling out more sauce. He heated up some garlic bread, sat down and watched me eat. No one came in. I ate and ate, and he gave me two cannoli and a cup of capuccino. He never accepted any money.

Night after night I sat in my little hole in the wall, drinking beer and listening to Walter Cronkite, who had stopped reciting the body count from the week's fighting in Vietnam, describe how Viet Cong sappers blasted a hole in the wall around the American embassy, then scrambled inside the embassy compound itself. Tough house-to-house fighting in Hue city, but the Marines were driving the North Vietnamese out. Saigon filled with dead and wounded, young Americans, shirtless and sweating, tossing dead enemy soldiers into a slippery stiff heap. I stirred chicken hearts and rice into my electric frying pan. Roaches and black bugs dashed to and fro, probing the perimeter of my dinner. A helicopter took off across the t.v. screen, a net swinging under its belly, blood spraying, body parts dropping, heading toward the South China Sea to feed the sharks. Snow dusted MacDougal Street. I huddled beside the t.v., eating chicken hearts, watching humans slaughter one another ten thousand miles away. The Year of Our Lord, 1968. The month of January. And the light at the end of the tunnel, the beacon Defense Secretary McNamara claimed was burning ever so brightly, had gone out.

Next to my room, a hippie clan dropped acid, smoked dope, and played *The Doors* and *Jefferson Airplane* night and day. When I walked to the toilet, which was right across from them, I could hear their hallucinations and their group gropings. Chairs crashed, dishes broke, they sang *Go Ask Alice* in loud squeaky voices. Sometimes I thought I heard them weeping.

I walked the streets at night, as I had done for the past six years, wandering along the Bowery, drifting through Washington Square Park, criss-crossing the Lower East Side. Alfie had quit the Old Reliable to work for the mafia, opening gay bars in Greenwich Village, but when the gumbahs asked him to turn an uptown restaurant into an S & M club he refused. "I told them they were all repressed faggots," he laughed. "Said they'd be a lot happier if they came out of the closet and stopped exploiting the gay crowd. Real men, my ass. Big guns, little dicks. Denial, that's their problem. I tell you, half the men I've slept with in the past five years have been 'straight' guys from New Jersey. Come to New York to get treated like women, want to get buggered so they can go back home and *pretend* to be men. It's so pathetic." Shortly after this, Alfie went into hiding.

The last time I saw him alive, he was living on St. Mark's Place with a new Puerto Rican lover. We sat in a circle, listening to a woman play the guitar and sing cowboy songs. I didn't like country western music, but the woman's voice was extraordinary, loud and haunting, cacophonous and sweet, and we sat for hours, Alfie passing around "poppers" and the woman, who had been crashing at Alfie's for a few weeks, guzzling bourbon, smoking joint after joint, and telling bawdy stories about growing up in Texas. One night she drained another bottle, took one last hit off the roach Alfie was passing around, and laid her guitar aside.

"I'm a goin' home to Texas to see my mama," she said. "Then I'm goin' out to California and get famous."

We laughed, and wished her well, because we weren't goin' home to see our mamas, but we were all tracking fame and fortune, hoping to find it just around the corner from Stanley's or Tompkins Square Park or the Old Reliable. Her name was Janis Joplin, and hey, Janis, thanks for the free concerts, wherever you are.

I searched for Julie Trees, so diminutive, so absurdly quiet, the leaves of her oak tree unmoving and her half-closed eyes slightly mocking, the empty syringe hanging from her thigh the last time we lay on a broken-down bed in a slumlord hotel, drinking Thunderbird laced with Mescaline, the room filling with heliotropic water and schools of psychedelic fish swimming round and round my head.

"I'm an apparition," she said. "A spectre, Cowboy. Just the window of your imagination. Your wet dream come true. A shadow you'll never catch."

Passing Siobhan's old building, stopping in at the Vazac and Stanley's for a drink, looking into the Old Reliable, and standing in front of the Cafe La Mama and Le Metro, but seeing no one I knew. Walking over to the Church-in-the-Bowery, hoping to find a sign announcing that Mulford would be reading there, wishing I could hear him "get down" on the white devil, the Vietnam War, slumlords, prisons, the PO-lice.

I sat in Tompkins Square Park, waiting for Zarro a.k.a.

Bilbo Baggins to appear, trying to conjure Catherine and John and even Willy J., but no one showed and the streetlights flickered, turning the park into a patchwork quilt of malice.

"Cronkite," laughed the veteran I was buying drinks for one night in the Vazac. "That clusterfuck, that chickenshit little clown. You don't really believe anything he says, do you? He's just a cog, man. They wind him up and he chirps numbers out of some general's hat. Alice-in-Fuckup-Land, that's what it is over there, man. That's Vietnam. Total fucking make-believe. Only this ain't no kids' story. This is body bags stuffed full of dumb dead sockhoppers. True fucking believers like I was. No shit. I was. I ate that shit for breakfast, lunch, and dinner. Gobbled it up. John Wayne and all those other fuckin' actors playin' war. All of it. Every bit of it. No fucking questions. Not for Johnny comes fucking home again a hero, man."

I bought the veteran another shot and a beer.

"I ain't lying," he said. "You think I'm lyin'? I was there, man. Twelve months humpin' the bush, twelve fuckin' months in-country. Killin' for God and L . . . fucking . . . B . . . fucking J. You think I don't know. I know. I fucking do know. So what the fuck they gonna do with me, cut my hair and send me back to Nam. I'd tell it to LBJ's fucking face if I ever saw him."

I bought him another round.

"When Cronkite says fifty American KIA, triple it. When he says a hundred, double it. At least that, maybe more. Shit, if you believe that clown we've killed every fucking NVA solider fifteen times in the last two years. None left. All KIA. But they're there. They're there all fucking right. And they're gonna be there. Gonna be RIGHT there. Like sprayin' cockroaches with Black Flag. Turn on the stove and more come out. More, and fucking more."

The bartender turned on the news and the veteran and I walked to the park where he sat with his eyes closed, taking deep angry tokes on a joint.

"Sometimes," he whispered, "I really wish I could just lie about the war. It would be a lot easier than tryin' to tell the truth. No one wants to hear what's really goin' down over there. No one cares. The truth is like a cactus, man. It grinds up your throat. But lies are like Twinkies, soooo easy to eat. It ain't World War II, that's for fuckin' sure. Thought it was, but it's not. Not gonna happen. Never gonna happen, that's all. And them dumb fuckin' assholes in Washington better get it fast, or we're all gonna be sorry, real fuckin' number 10, man. Sometimes, I wish they'd zippered me into one of them body bags, sent me home to get some rest."

I went back to my room, turned on the black and white t.v. and listened to the latest body count, not from Vietnam but the war on America's mean streets. Detroit was burning now, New York might be next. I wouldn't really be surprised, nor did I much care. Beryl had come and gone again. When she showed up at my door, thin, hollow-eyed, all her belongings in one small bag, I told her to get lost, but she refused to leave. Ten minutes passed, fifteen, twenty. I opened the door a crack and Beryl jammed it with her foot.

As we talked we removed our clothes, climbing naked onto my bouncy mattress and singing almost as loud as Jim Morrison in the pad next door, Beryl weeping as she often did during and after her orgasm, and we lay very still for a while warm and almost friendly in one another's arms. But we knew it was no good, that a thousand orgasms wouldn't help. We lay wrapped together and she told her lies, and I told mine, and one day I returned from the anti-poverty front to find a young man standing in my room and Beryl packing her meager belongings. The prince was wearing a black leather motorcycle jacket fringed with silver studs, a black motorcycle helmet was tucked under his arm. His Harley Davidson was parked almost on top of my bed and he looked hard into my eyes, but I just laughed in his face because I wasn't a kid anymore and it didn't matter; he couldn't hurt me and he couldn't see that I had expected him all along, had been waiting for him to appear, was delighted to see him ride away into the sunset with his princess who, spinning toward me as they were going out the door, declared:

"You'll never see me again, you bastard. This is the last time. The very last time. I know you don't believe me, but I really did love you and now I'm leaving forever." I laughed at her, too, knowing that Beryl, still far more beautiful than most Hollywood film stars, was just another shadow I'd been chasing and that I'd caught her too many times, she'd caught me too many times. I walked in to find her legs wrapped around other men, and she walked in to find other legs wrapped around me. I threw her to the wolves, she tossed me to the lions. I slapped her face, she smashed bottles over my head. I ripped her dress—the one she'd spent two weeks sewing—into shreds, she threw my typewriter into the air-shaft, flushed my poetry down the toilet.

Then we filled the tub with scalding water and lay soaking in a mound of bubble bath, laughing, lathering one another, locking together in one great giggling moaning coming cloud of suds, water splashing over the bathtub's sides and draining through the floorboards into the living room of the Hasidic Jewish family below us. We patted one another dry, sprinkled talcum powder over our pink warm skin, and curled together on clean sheets, sipping tea and whispering as though the ghosts in our bedroom, in us, might overhear our secrets, waking in the night, talking and making love again and again. But our marathon lovemaking, like our bouts of drinking, always ended. The world came lapping at our little nest. Sooner or later the landlord would tape the third eviction notice to our door, Con Edison would shut off our lights and cooking gas, the phone would go dead, our favorite bar would refuse us any more credit. And just before the police arrived to throw us out we would pack our things, make love one more time and walk, homeless once more, into the streets. She would turn one corner, I another. Sometimes I wouldn't see her again for months.

Beryl's prince mounted his steed and she climbed on behind, lifting her long delicious legs into the stirrups. He kicked at the starter and the Harley coughed, roared, lept forward. I closed the door, opened a quart of beer and turned on the evening news, holding the television's wires together until the program was over.

When I tried to write poetry the words spread out across the page like fieldstones, lifeless and unmovable. I couldn't make them sing. Even when I was selling blood, panhandling, and curling up in junkie crash pads, I could summon the muse. But now, I sat in Dr. Penny's office (when the indexing job ended and I was very poor again I returned to the war on poverty), opening her dividend checks and scratching out lines of verse on the backs of envelopes which I wadded and tossed into the garbage.

The last time I saw Zarro, he called New York a "bummer," said the Lower East Side was a "down place" for hobbits, and declared Middle Earth defunct.

"Bilbo's dead, man," said Zarro, pacing in front of the bench on which I was sitting. "And poor little Frodo too. All the tiny people done split for the Haight, man. Warmer there. More peaceful. Better vibes altogether. This just ain't where it's at anymore. Too much freakiness. Nothin' shakin' at all. I loved Groovy, man. He was like my soul. My own soul. Beautiful cat. And they wasted him. Linda, too, man. Cat just took a brick and smashed in their heads, man. Didn't know how much love he was killin', didn't care I guess. I know they're happy in the next chakra, but I'm feeling down, way way down. Time for Zarro to split, man. Take old baby snake and hit the road. Everything is karma. You know that. The dance of God. Who am I to try to direct? I follow, man. And when the currents pick me up, I float. Wow. Like one huge everlasting trip . . . Coming till my brain drains. But listen here man, here's my latest poem:

> *Later for the dames.*
> *Flyin' home on cranes.*
> *Huggin' unicorn manes.*
> *Suckin' on the flames.*
> *Facto, man. Frodo will rise from the dead.*
> *Raise up his head. Give us more bread.*
> *Handin' back the ring.*
> *So we all can do our thing.*
> *Goin' with the flow.*
> *Naked on the snow.*
> *I go. I go . . . with the karmic flow . . ."*

"Well, goodbye, Zarro," I said, shaking his hand. "I'll probably still be here when you get back."

"Not coming back, bro. Gonna hang in the sun, have some fun."

"I'll miss seeing you around here," I said.

"You're so BADDDD," Zarro laughed. "Never could quite get your case down. You and Julie Trees, man. Strange cats. Like hipsters, man. Like Lady and Master Hardrock. But cool, very cool. I dig your vibes, man. Always dug 'em. Knew you were good for a handout any time, any time you weren't lookin' for one yourself."

"Maybe you'll get lucky, Zarro."

"Oh man," Zarro sang, strumming his invisible guitar. "Get lucky. I was born lucky lucky. I got lucky teeth, man. A lucky nose. Lucky ears. The hair that grows on my head and between my legs is lucky. You're lookin' at lucky. Lucky hands, lucky feet, lucky eyes, lucky knees, lucky dick, lucky balls, lucky soul, brother. You want luck, I'll send you luck."

"Yeah, Zarro, send me a box of luck. I could always use it."

"You got it my man. Luck on the hoof. I'll send you a trainload, soon as I get my ass settled in the Haight. Little woman. Some good doobie. Some fine sounds. Don't take much to make us hobbits happy. Not much at all."

"I don't know," I laughed, "never been a hobbit."

"When you wish upon a star," Zarro sang.

"Take care of yourself, Zarro."

"You too man, you too."

I sat in the park circling like a wolf after some familiar yet ever so faint scent, trailing back over the years. I had gone to the welfare office and asked to see a worker. Six hours later a young woman waved me into her cubicle.

"Listen," I said. "I really can't stand living like this anymore."

"Yes," she said. "Like what?"

"Like poor, drunk, never having a place to live. Always wondering whether I'm going to survive from day to day."

"Yes."

"I'd like to go back to school, and was wondering if you could help me."

"You mean the welfare department?"

"Yes."

"Are you receiving public assistance right now?"

"No."

"Have you ever received public assistance—surplus food, a clothing allowance, things like that?"

"No."

"Are you working?"

"Sometimes. I have a drinking problem."

"Are you an alcoholic?"

"I don't know."

"But you do work?"

"Sometimes."

"Do you have a place to live?"

"I live with friends. Or in the streets."

"Do you have an address right now?"

"Kind of."

"Have you ever been psychotic?"

"No. I've been in psychiatric facilities, but they never said I was crazy."

"Could you get one of those places to write us saying that you had been certifiably insane?"

"No, I wasn't insane."

"Well, I'm sorry. If you could get someone to delcare that you were once psychotic, then perhaps we could find some way to help you. We do have a program for returning students, but the rules . . ."

"You mean the only way you can help me is if I can prove I've been insane?"

"Yes, that's right."

"That's the only way?"

"Yes."

"Even if I have no money, no family, no home?"

"Yes."

I sat in Tompkins Square Park, drifting in and out of the past, unable to project a future, watching kids who came to the city for a happy hit and got one—arms measled with needle tracks, skin like old newsprint, eyes locked permanently on vacant. Watching the parade, seeing my own reflection, and wondering if we would be forgotten. Would the city of New York erect a statue in Tompkins Square Park to the unknown flower child? Kids like Groovy and Linda who thought their own good vibes could deliver them from evil, and wound up getting clubbed to death by a junkie in a basement on Avenue B. Would famous speed freaks like Julie Trees and acid heads like Zarro leave their handprints in the park's sidewalks? And might future generations find a bronze plaque stating that:

On October 4, 1958, Archibald J. Hendricks, the very first beatnik to arrive on the Lower East Side, sat on this bench and smoked a joint.

Would the parks department construct a special little cemetery, with headstones shaped like hashpipes, listing the names of beatniks and hippies killed in action in the East Village?

Watching my own reflection pass by I felt a strange new passion to stay alive. I wanted to swim out of the undertow of romantic suffering that had pulled, and was still pulling, so many of us under. We had made a cult out of death, turning Hart Crane, Sylvia Plath, Dylan Thomas, and others into idols. We wanted to balance on the razor's edge, to look clearly and fearlessly into the abyss, to die young and misunderstood. If our lives were genuinely tragic, they would make sense. If we suffered enough, we would be remembered. But I had danced too many times with death, slipping away just before the music ended, the escape beating through my veins like a hotshot of speed. I was tired of participating in my own demise. It just didn't make sense any more. If we had run away from families who put us in jail and locked us up in snakepits back in Ohio and California and Iowa, then why were we killing ourselves in the Big Apple?

"Someday," Dr. Maynard had said, "you will want to see those great lightning flashes out over the plains again. You'll want to take a clump of that black earth in your hands and roll it around, feeling the magic of it, the strength, the difference between it and concrete."

We were sitting in the recreation room at Clarion State Mental Hospital. Patients circled like lost camels round and round the room. The pool table listed on three legs, cues broken, pockets ripped open. The ping-pong set had disappeared weeks ago. An old man stopped, staring at me for a long time. "Give me cigarette," he demanded. I removed one from my pack, lighted it for him. He stood very still, drawing smoke into his legs, smiling. "Fuck you. Fuck you you god-damn sonofabitch," he screamed, rejoining the camel herd.

"That's when the pain will come," Dr. Maynard continued. "Not when you're out there trying to survive, living on anger, hating. But one day when you wake up and look out the window, like I did years ago, and wish you could smell spring again, wishing you could walk beside a stream and watch little patches of ice start to break up and flow away, and there's winter wheat poking up through the snow, a family of crows eating corn, the sky so blue you suffer a kind of panic. That's when it's going to hurt. Because you won't have anywhere to go. Home will be inside your chest, in your heart and you'll feel the pull, like a bird feeling the time has come to migrate again, but knowing its wings have been clipped and it must stay behind until they heal. Heal, do you hear how it sounds, the word 'heal'?"

"Bad poetry," Julie Trees would have shouted. "Romantic drivel. Soybean Keats. Haystack Wordsworth. Cornbelt metaphysics."

I wished she were there beside me on that park bench, lighting up the night with her vitriolic commentary. I would have liked to press our boney frames together one last time, riding some small crest of pleasure.

I sat in Tompkins Square park for days, and late one night a group of Puerto Rican kids came prancing and laughing and owning the world and I stood with my back against the wall of the pissoir, silently warning them **NOT TO GET TOO CLOSE TO ME/ NOT TO LOOK AT ME/ NOT TO FUCK WITH ME** and above this paranoic rumbling a little voice, clear as kindness, telling me that fear had driven me mad, urging me to leave before I injured or even killed someone.

I drove a screwdriver deep into the heart of my rat's nest mattress, nailed the windows shut, installed a set of new locks on the door, and flushed the keys down the toilet. Then I threw all of my belongings into a paper bag, bought a one-way ticket to a town in Pennsylvania, and left the old demon's friends a note:

DEAR NICE BOYS. I HOPE YOU ALL WIND UP IN
THE EAST RIVER WITH MANY LARGE HOLES IN
YOUR NICE HEADS.

"Do you speak French?" asked Mama, when I wandered
into Chez MaMa the next afternoon.
"Oh, oui oui," I said.
"Have you ever waited on tables in a French restaurant?"
"Oh, oui oui."
"What do you know about French cuisine?"
"*Beaucoup, Madame. Beaucoup.*"
"Darling," Mama drawled, squeezing lemon over the baby
squid on her plate and sipping from her glass of white wine.
"You are a terrible liar. You don't know French. You know
nothing about working in a French restaurant. You are a
stupid American who thinks French cuisine is French fries.
Ah, but you are a cute one. I like men with balls. So few of
them left anymore. Start this afternoon at 4:00. See Johnny.
He will show you what to do. Now leave so I can finish my
lunch."

The metal tray, stacked high with plates of mushroom-
capped filet mignon, steaming tins of escargot, langoustine,
and scampi in garlic butter sauce, is breaking my shoulder.
I must set it down, must distribute the food, but I dare not.
"Darling," Mama shouted just a few nights ago, stopping
in the middle of her singing and pointing one fat trembling
finger at a new waiter, "you are fired, darling." The poor boy,
not hearing or simply not understanding, continued setting
out plates of "Mama's Chicken with Papa's Stuffing" (a half-
baked chicken setting astride a huge sausage) until Mama
grabbed his collar and bellowed, "No no no, darling. *Vous etes
fini.* Get out of my house. Now."
Mama sings on and on, swaying her elephantine torso to
the beat, blowing kisses into her corpulent hands, while waiters and waitresses stand at attention, holding trays aloft on
wobbly arms.
Candles flickering inside red and yellow glass bubbles; couples holding hands across checkered tablecloths; forks poised

above plates of clams casino, marinated mussels, stuffed artichokes. Mama wails about love lost, or found, in gay Paris.
Out of her sight, a waiter pops the cork on a bottle of champagne, swaddling the bottle in a white napkin, softly crunch-
ing it into a silver ice bucket. The Delaware River stretches
flat and unmoving like an endless strip of black plastic. Fish
rise toward the moon, mid-air sparks holding, holding, going out.

When Mama stops singing, I glide from table to table with
my partner, Johnny. Our knee-length denim aprons are
clean and starched, crisp white napkins are draped over
our wrists.

"*Oui, Madame,*" says Johnny, bowing and pretending to
speak French, "*Voulez-vous aimer votre diner?*" The couple
smiles and nods, not really understanding.

"I mean," he says, pouring the last drops of wine into their
glasses, "are you quite *fini?* Finished with your," pausing just
at the edge of contempt, "*dîn . . . ne?*"

"Oh yes," the man replies, "I guess Mrs. Melville and I are
done, waiter."

"Well, not quite, waiter," the woman adds. "I think Dr. Melville might want to have a little after-dinner drink, wouldn't
you dear?"

"That would be lovely," Dr. Melville says. "Yes, I think we'll
have a Grand Manrnier this evening."

"Grand Marnier. *Oui. Oh oui oui, Monsieur.*" Johnny chants.
"Oh, beaucoup parfait," rolling his eyes and bowing once
more as he reaches across the table to pick up first the man's,
and then the woman's entree dish, holding them up for in-
spection before tossing them into the canal that separates
Chez Mama from the river.

"Oh my God," the man chuckles. "Look what you did. You
threw our plates into the water."

"*Oui, monsieur,*" Johnny says, sailing coffee cups, desert
dishes, knives forks and spoons into the river. "*Oui. Vous êtes
très idiotic.*"

The couple giggle.

"*Fermez la bouche,*" Johhny grins. "*Et fou trois very much.*"

The dinner plates hover on the water's surface for a moment before sinking, silently, away. Dr. and Mrs. Melville gig-

gle. Johnny removes their tablecloth, wads it into a ball, and tosses it away. He replaces the cloth with a new one, orders a busboy to reset the table with ashtray, water glasses, and coffee cups, and we stroll away.

We swing through the kitchen doors, knocking into waiters and waitresses, pushing busboys and busgirls aside. The kitchen floor is covered with grease. Bits of celery, lettuce leaves, and coffee grounds float in pools of dirty water. A busboy slips and goes down in a tray-clanking dish-smashing heap. No one stops to help him. Johnny surfs toward the counter where waiters and waitresses are screaming orders. Everyone is jostling for position, snapping limp yellow order slips on and yanking slips off a wire that runs in front of the stoves. Chefs push the slips forward with giant knives. Flames leap from gas grills, frying pans bubble. Chefs slam dishes onto the counter in front of the wait-staff. "Garnish," they scream. "Parsley, not celery, you shoemaker." Dishwashers scrape food from plates, tossing cups and forks and saucers into metal racks, slamming the racks into and out of steaming machines. Cups break. Escargot holders fly. Coffee spills. Steaks, frog legs, and lobster tails slide off plates and wait-staff pick them up, wipe them off on their aprons, and throw them back on their plates.

It is Saturday night, 110 degrees in the kitchen, and getting hotter. Mama doesn't allow any of her guests to be seated until they've had drinks at the bar and then, with a grand wave of her hand, the stampede for tables begins. Within five minutes all three dining rooms are packed. Menus snap open, busboys scramble to fill glasses, waiters scribble orders, and Mama strolls through the chaos, smiling and waving as though this were yet another opening night. She hires too few waiters and waitresses, never enough bus-help, pays us three dollars for an eight-hour shift. I grab a half-filled martini glass from the dishwashers' heap and slug down the contents, slurp an Old Fashion from another glass, chase it with coffee. A new waitress, just back from college in Vermont, stands in the middle of the kitchen, her eyes rolling toward heaven, her hands shaking, tears dripping down her cheeks. No one stops to help her. Our shirts and blouses and aprons cling to our backs. Sweat chews at our eyes. We wade through a world of steam.

"Goddamn it, you shoemaker," one of the chefs shouts at a young waiter who is close to tears. "Don't tell me you ordered langoustine. I know what you put up here. You ordered pepper steak. That's what you get, pepper steak."

"No," the waiter cries, "I ordered langoustine."

The cook is drunk. He waves a long knife, takes a great slug from a container of rum, gin, orange juice, lemon juice, and vodka, and hurls the steak back onto the grill. He wipes the plate clean with his apron, scatters garnish and fills it with langoustine.

"Here you shoemaker, get out of my sight."

Waiters and waitresses slam their trays onto the counter, arranging parsley and bits of citrus fruit on their plates, exchanging gossip and complaints.

"Those old bitches at table 3 tried to stiff me, can you believe that? Left me a dollar and twenty cents. I gave it right back to them. 'Here,' I said, 'you obviously need this more than I do.'"

"So Mr. MacAndrews at table 7 sticks his middle finger in the coffee, as he always does, then holds it up and says: 'Hey waiter, you got a doggie bag for my wife's pussy? Ha Ha Ha.' Real class, that one."

"And that little swish at table 9, the one who claims he's Batman one week, Lawrence Welk the next. You see what he picked up in Philly? Jesus, robbing the cradle I'd say. So, when he calls in he tries to disguise his voice, says he wants reservations for himself, the ambassador to Greece, and his son. Great tipper, though, even if he is a flaming queen."

"See that couple at table 10. The leather chick, and Mr. America. Yeah, I swear she's reachin' under the table and playin' with him. Johnny brings her steak and she sends it back, says it's not done well enough. He tells Pierre to kill it, really dead this time. Puts it back on the table, burned to shit, looks like a briquette. Jesus, you should have seen the look on her face."

Busboys and girls rush back and forth, screaming at the dishwashers. "We need soup spoons. We gotta have shrimp forks. Where the hell are the lobster crackers. Jesus Christ, how the hell are we supposed to set up the tables without anything?"

"Shut your face," the teenage dishwashers scream back. "We're doing the best we can. We're human beings, goddamn it. Hey, get us a beer and we'll go faster."

Johnny and I fill our trays with salads and hors d'oeuvres, ignoring the pleas and threats, brush down our hair, wipe our faces off on a clean dish towel, throw the towel at the dishwashers, fill our pockets with extra shrimp and escargot forks, pop a couple of shrimp into our mouths and walk back through the double doors to the terrace. Maurice Chevalier croons *April in Paris,* the candles flicker, a fish leaps toward heaven, and Dr. and Mrs. Melville depart, leaving Johnny Q. and me a very substantial tip.

Mama feeds the wait-staff fly-specked casseroles left over from brunch, forces us to give the bartenders ten percent of our tips—they ignore us when they get busy hustling their own customers. She abuses us in front of our customers, and fires waiters and waitresses almost every night. I can't understand all this, but when I try to talk to other wait-staff I am warned not to even use the word "union." "Restaurant owners in this valley hate that word, particularly Mama," says one old waiter. "She'll fire you just for *thinking* about organizing a union."

One lunch shift I am called to wait on Mama, a fate every one of us dreads because her appetite is voracious and insatiable. Lunch lasts for hours, each dish meticulously prepared by the chefs and delivered, without flaw, to her own special table. I deliver a bottle of Pouilly Fusse, chilled to Mama's specifications, wrapped in a starched white towel and inserted into a silver ice bucket. I time her baby squid perfectly, forgetting none of the accoutrements she expects to go with it. She smiles and nods her approval. I bring her soft-shell crabs, arranged in a semicircle, with six wedges of lemon sliced exactly one-eighth-inch thick. I place the stuffed artichokes and a plate of mussels three inches to the left of her dinner plate, order the pantryman to lightly brown her bread and cut it into four-inch strips, screaming at him for putting too much oil and vinegar on her salad, warning him to sprinkle exactly *eight* croutons over her lettuce, and to rest a lemon wedge on each side of the bowl. Mama smiles, sips her wine, devours dish after dish. My own customers must wait. I dash in and out of the kitchen. The cooks stop yelling at me. The wait-staff winks, smirks, shrugs their support. I grind Mama's very own Colombian beans, polish her silver creamer, set down a slice of cheesecake, and flourish the coffeepot high above the table, allowing steaming liquid to cascade into her cup, filling it to exactly one-half-inch below the rim without spilling a drop. I brush crumbs from the table, fill her water glass, deftly remove the wine bucket. Mama folds her hands over her huge stomach, pleased and ever so content.

"Darling," she says. "That was *tres bonne. Magnifique. Vous êtes un grand garçon.* But darling," still smiling, "you are fired. We never had a fucking union here. We won't ever have one. Over my dead body, darling. Please leave my house at once."

I walked into the kitchen, tossed off my apron, and said goodbye to Molly, the old black woman who had worked in Mama's kitchen for twenty years, mixing plates of *Moules Mama,* stuffing artichokes, peeling fifty million shrimp a week, working with a quiet, methodical dignity, and never raising her voice to anyone, not even on Saturday nights when the cooks insulted and threatened waiters, waitresses wept and walked out in the middle of serving a table of ten, busboys and busgirls threw trayloads of dishes into the canal, and dishwashers got so drunk they broke more cups than they washed.

I told Molly that I was going back to school, and she shook her head and laughed with such kindness that I blinked back tears. Molly wouldn't run for office, teach school, act in a film, or write a book. She wouldn't lead men into battle, or make a lot of money. There would never be a statue in the town's little park to this beautiful and very dignified black woman. Molly would work in Mama's kitchen until she got old and tired, but not defeated.

I walked out of Mama's and strolled along the tow path that ran along the canal. Water bubbled over stones in the river and a mallard with six little ducklings floated downstream, quacking and bobbing their heads in and out of the water. Kathleen would soon arrive from Connecticut, where she worked as a live-in nanny and taught French at an academy for girls. We would stroll through town, holding hands and looking into the windows of little curio shops. After dinner we might go for a drive through the countryside or a hike in the woods, picking violets or lying together by a stream.

I rented a room for $12.50 a week in a colonial inn with walk-in fireplaces, open-beam ceilings, random wide-width plank floors, and we would lie in bed sipping wine and listening to the rain and telling stories, slipping into a soft springtime sleep. When I awoke in the night gnashing my teeth or screaming, Kathleen rocked me in her arms, trying to quiet my fears. I locked the door to my room, secured the windows, kept a knife under my bed, and often lay wide-eyed listening and waiting.

We drove into the city and sat in Tompkins Square Park. The babushkas huddled together on their benches. Dogs romped, pigeons pecked, squirrels wagged their mischievous tails. Barefoot flower children, some with children of their own, strummed guitars and sang Bob Dylan, Phil Ochs, Dave Von Ronk, Buffy St. Marie. We walked the streets, the setting still intact, the script unchanged, even the same music, yet something was missing. I wanted to run the film in reverse, to get back inside its happy dangerous action, but I knew Zarro was right. The fun part walked off the night Linda and Groovy were lured into a basement on Avenue B, thinking their own good vibes could outshine Willy J. Lizard and his soul-dead pushers. Guns. Knives. Sticks. Stones. More lizards. More cops. More sad-faced suburban couples cruising the streets in big shiny cars, searching for sons and daughters who'd fallen ankle, ass, or neck-deep into the East Village. More teary-eyed moms and dads posting hand-lettered signs, "Come home, Suzie, Come home Johh, we love and miss you so much" (with a photograph of their lost child) on the walls outside hippie haunts.

We went deeper into my old neighborhood, stopping into bars where, throwing down whiskey shots, I managed to hold the past in the palm of my hand. Drunk and dangerously maudlin, I informed Kathleen that the only cure for slumlords is public execution, that cops deserved to get shot, and that Mulford ("Mulford who?") was right, the white man is a devil and he's gonna get what's comin' to him, what's coming to us.

"But landlords are human," insisted Kathleen.

"No, they're not. They're mass murderers."

"The police have families too."

"So what? Tell that to the people they beat up and torture every day."

"Besides, you're not black."

"Not on the outside."

"Stop fooling yourself."

"About what?"

"About being something you're not."

I wept for days when Martin Luther King was assassinated, accusing Kathleen of being a racist because she didn't share my pain. I shouted that the American people ought to overthrow the government. She thought it might be better to vote. I said Malcolm X was a greater man than John Kennedy, greater than any president of the United States would ever be. She thought not. I declared that Richard Nixon was committing genocide in Vietnam. She was opposed to the war, but thought I was too strident. We crossed the Mississippi one sunny afternoon, the radio blasting *Just Like a Rollin' Stone,* a can of beer in my lap and a crushing fear in my lungs. I wanted to return to my home state, to my hometown, and to my kin, knowing that exile was a condition of the heart, not a matter of where I might live. I wanted to forgive my family, even though I hadn't begun to forgive myself. There had been, and there would be, many years of rage and self-pity and guilt and defeat and doubt and trying to go home only to flee again, soaked up in caffeine and dexadrine and the rush of packing and driving into the night through rain and snow, past a burning Greyhound bus on its side in the ditch and trucks dangling off an overpass and hallucinogenic rabbits in the headlights, six-foot-high shadows waving their paw-arms in our faces. I wanted the center line, clean and yellow and pulling us from Iowa to New Mexico, to Arkansas back up the coast to Montreal, and down again, living in a tent, carrying a gun, drinking, always drinking, trying to find some shadow that might keep us together—until one day we had to call it even and, without K., I started the long climb back to the person I might have been and wouldn't ever be and thought I really was. Back, away, from chasing shadows.

CHAPTER 12

Home

The water looks back at me, reflecting starched white shirt, creased black slacks. A slight rolling coil. Nervous spring, even when standing still. Ears pricked, nose testing the breeze, the Iowa river just another mean street, another hallway in some cuckoo bin. The mirror shimmers, cracks, drifts in and out of focus. Ten years, a decade of my life, floating downstream with the first leaves of autumn. I see Julie Trees at campus rallies. Black beret. Patchwork Levis ripped, precisely, to expose one freckled knee. Bandoliers of peace symbols. Dancing snake hair. My arms around her, and I'm laughing.

"Got the monkey off your back, Julie?"

"Let me tell you, brother," she says, adjusting her beret. "Revolution comes from the barrel of a gun. Not some motherfuckin' nickel bag."

"Right on, Julie."

"Right on, my brother."

Zarro mounts the podium, wearing shades and a daishiki, waving a copy of Mao's *Little Red Book*. Squatting on the roof of the physics building, FBI agents adjust their long-range lenses, snap on their tape recorders, waiting for the speaker to lash out against imperialism and capitalism and genocide. Wild applause. Raised fists. **Right on bro. Tell it like it is.**

Power to the people. Up against the wall, motherfucker.
Alfie dances by, barefoot, flowers in his hair, singing something about Hare and Krishna, throwing candy kisses to the
student revolutionaries who cluster about Zarro. I hear my
old friends' voices, feel their presence, but when I reach out
to touch them, they are shadows.

The moon rises red and full over the Iowa River, the windows of our Quonset hut twinkle with stars. I drift off to
sleep listening to an owl's soft hooting, but our cat stirring
in its basket startles me awake, the moon changing shape
frightens me out of bed, blankets scatter across the floor, torn
sheets and pillows land in corners. In the morning, shadows
crochet soft patterns on the walls, sunlight raises the shades,
and children sing on their way to school. I sleep.

You lie in a cold white hospital room, plastic tubes stuck
into your arms, plastic tubes hissing gently beneath your
nose, your bladder draining into a clear plastic bag. Yawning,
moaning, your eyes sliding open. Comfortable? Affirmative.
Uncomfortable? Affirmative. See out the window? Affirmative. Not see out the window? Difficult little nods. A clot, say
the doctors, small and powerful enough to destroy the right
half of your body, to turn your tongue to stone, to paralyze
your vocal cords. Your daughters spot your cheeks with
rouge, brush back your thick, still curly, hair, wet your lips
with a towel, and color them with pink lipstick.

Closing my eyes, I imagine lying safe and warm after a
good dinner and the rain step-dancing on the roof and me
snuggling down with a family of squirrels or baby bunnies
in their storybook nest. "And the prince and princess lived
happily ever after, and everyone in the kingdom was happy
too." The war in Vietnam ended, but the kingdom didn't
celebrate. Brave ships didn't sail up rivers, hoisting flags and
blowing blood-red streamers from their cannons. Children
didn't turn into dragons, dancing pageants for intoxicated
warriors who, after the little dancers took off their masks
and squatted in a circle, would tell Homeric tales of adventure and courage and victory over dark forces. Samurai
didn't parade through the grateful streets of the kingdom,

singing and reciting epics. The prince and princess didn't ride off into eternal bliss.

The prince lies in Arlington Cemetery, an eternal flame burning over his grave, his brother sleeping forever beside him. John F. Kennedy, Martin Luther King, Malcolm X, Medgar Evers, Bobby Kennedy, Fred Hampton, George Jackson, Janis Joplin, Jimmy Hendrix, Jim Morrison, 58,000 American names on a black granite wall, 2,000,000 Vietnamese ghosts wandering the rice paddies and jungles and mangrove forests, skin still burning napalm, white phosphorous still boiling their brains, their arms still filled with shredded children, and in this country a lost generation, still trying to recover from an overdose of lies and deceit. The Sixties rode out not with a bang, not even with a whimper, but with the whump whump of a helicopter rising from the White House grounds, a grinning Howdy Doody in the doorway, waving Bye Bye to his favorite suckers. He wasn't Camelot, but no matter. There never had been one, not in Washington, D.C. anyway. No prince or princess. Just those who gots, and those who don't gots. In the United States of America, everyone starts out even. Some (shhhh now, keep it to yourself) with broken legs. Others (shhhhh, now, no one knows but us) on stilts.

If we could talk, what might we say to one another? I am your only son. Do you know me? You are my mother. Do I know you? You carried me in your womb. I suckled at your breasts. Your genes shape my eyes and mouth, the texture of my hair, the fairness of my skin. Mother. Son. DNA bonded, and yet . . . you played by the rules, you held your place, burying volcanic rage and paralyzing fear inside hypochondria, inside migraine headaches and angina attacks, inside depression. Who dealt your hand? Poverty, gender, class, all of the above. Our heritage, you said: "*A long line of horse thieves.*" Our anthem: "*You can't get ahead for losing.*" Our sense of place: "*On the wrong side of the tracks.*" You exploded, every single day of your life. Inside. Not out. Fire ran through your veins, yet your skin was soft and cool and dry, to touch, as the belly of a frog. Seismic flashes broke from your eyes, but friends and family saw only veils of tears.

Once upon a time you might have seen me off to tilt at windmills, to chase infidels across the desert, and wrest castles from the hands of evil trolls. You might have circled my neck with garlands of hyacinths and laid my father's magic-tested sword in my gallant arms. Bending to kiss your noble head, my horse rearing with impatience, I would have received your blessing and rode off to battle, carrying your tear-stained shawl as a talisman against injury or death. Once upon a time, before there were psychiatrists and loony bins and lobotomies and forced sterilization and shock treatments and lithium. Before the enchanted forest was clear-cut, before the knights of the square table got hooked on late-night HA HA, and before ladies in waiting turned tricks for fifteen minutes of fame.

I had hoped that I might tell you about chasing shadows, and I had feared that you might even read this book. For so many years I hid in the closet, not wanting people to know that I had been "observed and evaluated" on psychiatric wards, that I was given electro-shock treatments, that I was an alcoholic, that I once cut my wrists, that the army didn't want me, nor I them, that I am, and always will be, "an ex-mental patient." I sit beside your bed, tears falling into my lap, listening to the soft drip drip of your bladder, my father's tears, the nurses chatter down the hall, the subdued buzz of a soap opera on the overhead screen. I am crying because I know, now, that my quest for freedom meant, to you, the very definition of your prison. Watching me grow to manhood filled you with dread, not just for my own safety, but for your own fragile sanity. You locked me up in psychiatric wards to keep from seeing the bars behind which you ate and slept and went to church and waited for a God that had left you, an intelligent, sensitive, and enraged woman, without an exit. In the interstices of your buried hope, you dreamed of other possibilities, but when you saw your own reflection in the shadow of my flight, you dug into your quiver, sprung your bow, and aimed for your son's wild, tameless heart.

I went so far down I couldn't see a shard of up, yet in the streets of San Francisco and New York, I saw all too clearly. No goals. No models of reality. No rhetorical constructs. Just what is and isn't on the block, what was, and wasn't, in my heart and head. Diving bell loneliness. Fear-gut hunger. Night sticks. Vomit. Pot. Amphetamine. Knives. Guns. Orgasms. Blood. Gratuitous kindness. Creative cruelty. "Freedom's just another word for nothing left to lose," wailed Janis Joplin. Down to licking the mustard off the sidewalk, it's easy to discover what she means. Climbing Mt. Sisyphus, a twenty-year trek after leaving the city, it was always good to have Janis along, especially when the going got rough and it seemed like there might not be a reachable summit, which, it turns out, there isn't.

Storybook mornings when I was a prince and you my royal princess, walking by an enchanted woods sprinkled with wildflowers and magic frogs, my hand in yours. "Listen," you would say, "they're saying hello to you, Freddy. The frogs are telling you good morning." "Good morning Froggie Woggie," I would shout, loving them with the passion of a four-year-old. We rode the streetcar to the butcher's shop, chatting away while he plucked the chicken clean and wrapped it, still warm, in brown paper. We had lunch in Bishop's cafeteria, gazed into great aquariums filled with candy, giggled up and down the new escalator in Yonkers department store.

The funeral home is filled to overflowing, banks of flowers beneath your casket, long, breathless weeping. I hold my arm around my father's boney shoulders, patting his eighty-one-year-old back. He bends to kiss you, but you do not open your eyes. I touch your face, and you do not respond. You always believed I would come home, that your grandchildren would bounce through the door after school, as I once did, carrying flowers from a neighbor's yard, that we would celebrate holidays, share the gift of life.

I had hoped to tell you about my exile. Perhaps we would go for a long walk, shed tears, complete our circle. A bitter, unseasonable wind slaps our faces as we climb the slope toward the site where you will be lowered into the earth. We sit on metal chairs, rubbing our hands together, crying. A man reads from the Bible. I do not know him. He reads on, his own hands shaking in the cold. Snow sweeps into our faces. Water freezes in the corners of our eyes. We descend the hill, my father slipping to his knees in the snow. I help him to his feet, and we kiss friends and relatives goodbye, squeeze hands, goodbye.

Perhaps we will have our talk some day. I will put my arms around you, tell you that I love you, something I could not do, even when you lay in your cold white hospital bed, drifting somewhere between life and death. The universe expands, contracts, our planet spins on its axis. We are born, we live, we die. The rest is mystery, the great dance of the universe. I accept it, embrace it, am grateful for the time I have left to sing its wonders.

Rest, my mother, in peace.

NO END.